Caledonia Ontario Now in Colour Photos, Saving Our History One Photo at a Time

Photography
by Barbara Raué
©2018

Series Name:
Cruising Ontario

Book 36: Caledonia

Cover photo: 68 Edinburgh Square

Series Name: Cruising Ontario
The Authority on Saving Our History One Photo at a Time in colour photos

Book 33: Southampton
Book 34: Jarvis
Book 35: Hagersville
Book 36: Caledonia
Book 37: Simcoe
Book 38: Cambridge Part 1 - Galt Book 1
Book 39: Cambridge Part 1 - Galt Book 2
Book 40: Cambridge Part 2 - Preston
Book 41: Cambridge Part 3 - Hespeler
Book 42: Kitchener Book 1
Book 43: Kitchener Book 2
Book 46: Shelburne
Book 47: Alton, Mono and Caledon
Book 48: London in Colour
Book 50: Orangeville Beginnings in Colour
Book 51: Orangeville on Broadway in Colour
Book 52: Orangeville Book 3 in Colour
Book 53: Dundas in Colour Book 1
Book 54: Dundas in Colour Book 2
Book 55: Dundas in Colour Book 3
Book 56: Stratford
Book 57: Hanover
Book 58: New Hamburg Book 1
Book 59: New Hamburg Book 2 and Haysville
Book 60: Waterdown in Colour
Book 61: Burlington in Colour

Caledonia is a small riverside community located on the Grand River in Haldimand County. It is located at the intersection of Highway 6 and Highway 54 (within the town, these streets are called Argyle Street and Caithness Street respectively). On Highway 6, the town is 10 kilometers south of Hamilton and 10 kilometers north of Hagersville. On Highway 54, the town is 15 kilometers east of Brantford and 10 kilometers west of Cayuga.

The Grand River flows 293 kilometres from the Dundalk Highlands to Lake Erie and is the largest river in southern Ontario. The river winds its way through marshes, woods, farmsteads, and communities. Rainbow trout use this river in their migration.

Caledonia was once a small strip of land between Seneca and Oneida villages. The Grand River traveled through Caledonia dividing it into two sides, North and South. In 1834, Ranald McKinnon was hired to build a dam in Seneca and a dam in Caledonia. Completed in 1840, the dams made water power available. The dam at Caledonia was constructed as part of a series of dams, locks and canals to facilitate navigation of the Grand River from Lake Erie to Brantford. Mills were built throughout Seneca village, and five mills were built in Caledonia by 1850. Commercial navigation ceased by 1879, but the dam continued to serve the local mills and provided a recreation opportunity. The present dam was built in 1980 downstream of the original structure.

Table of Contents

Argyle Street   Page 5

Orkney Street   Page 19

Sutherland Street   Page 22

Inverness Street   Page 27

Caithness Street   Page 29

Edinburgh Square   Page 49

Banff Street   Page 53

Architectural Terms   Page 58

Caledonia's Building Styles   Page 61

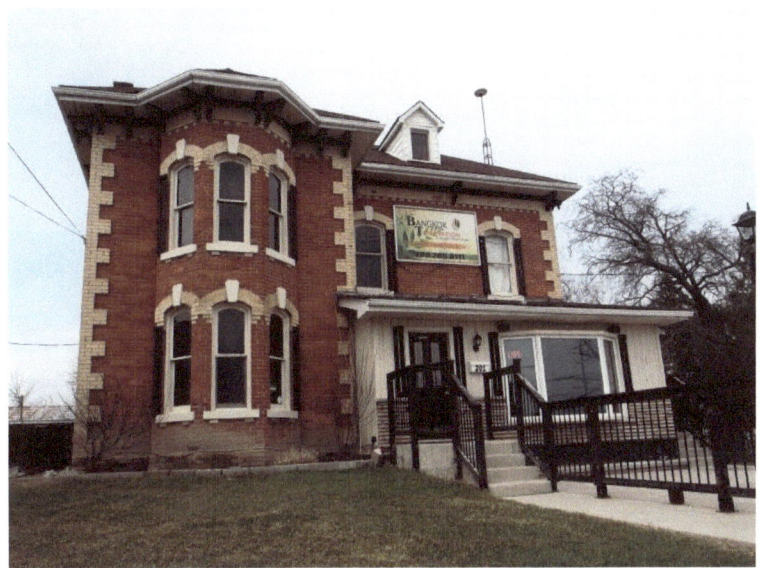

201 Argyle Street – Italianate, hipped roof, dormer in attic, corner quoins, keystones and voussoirs, dichromatic brickwork, dentil moulding under cornice, paired brackets

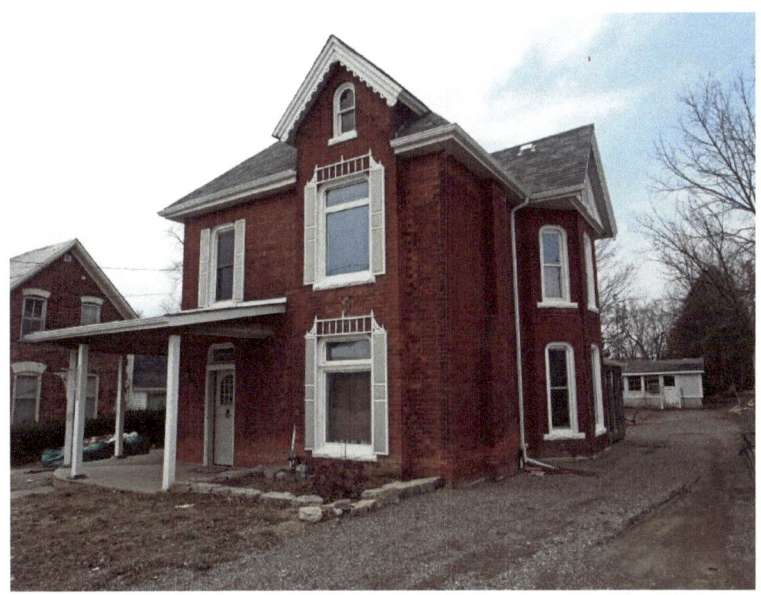

159 Argyle Street – Italianate with two-and-a-half storey frontispiece, verge board trim on gable, two-storey bay window on side

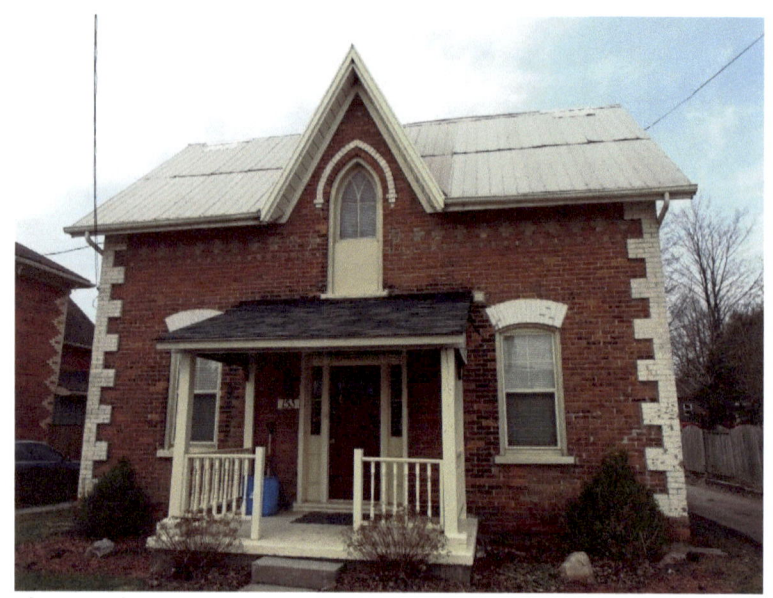

153 Argyle Street – Gothic Revival cottage, corner quoins, decorative brickwork

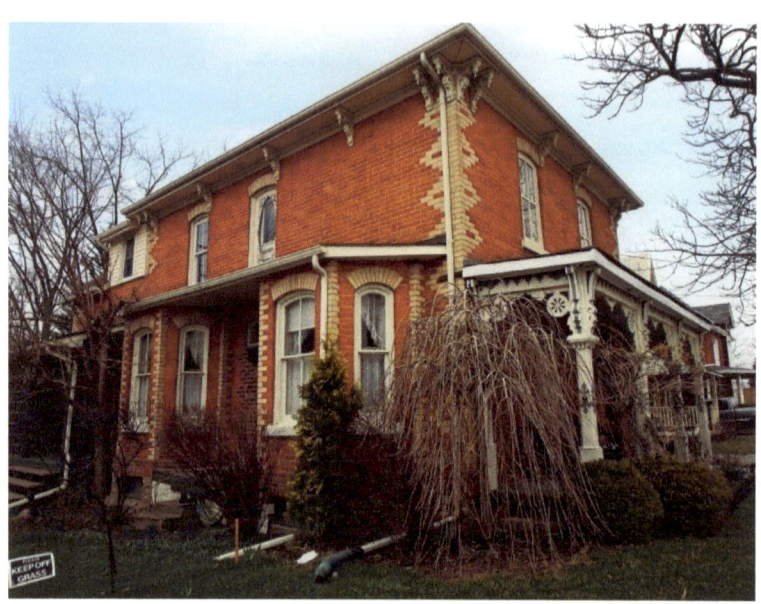

149 Argyle Street – Italianate – cornice brackets, dichromatic brickwork, corner quoins

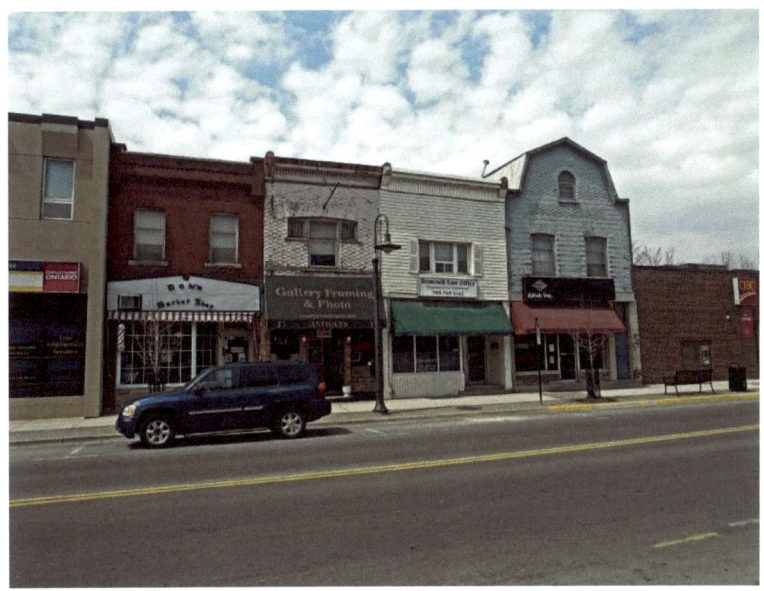

15-21 Argyle Street

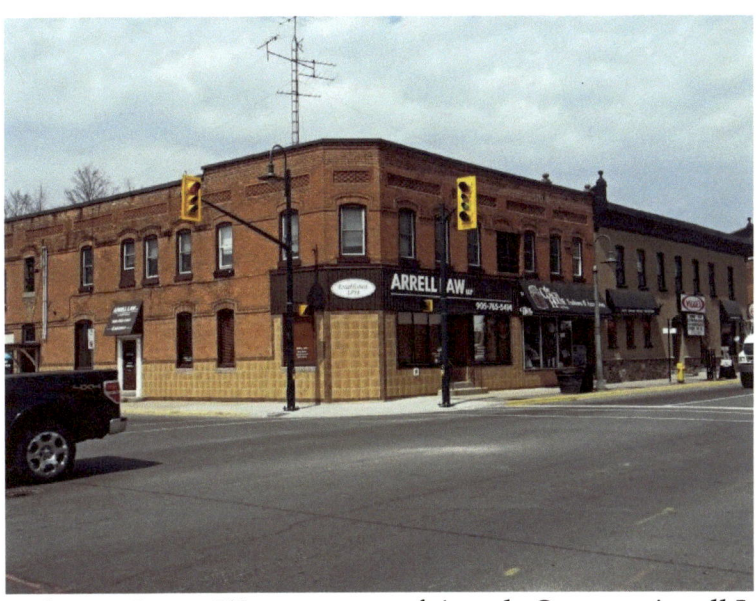

2 Caithness Street West, corner of Argyle Street – Arrell Law

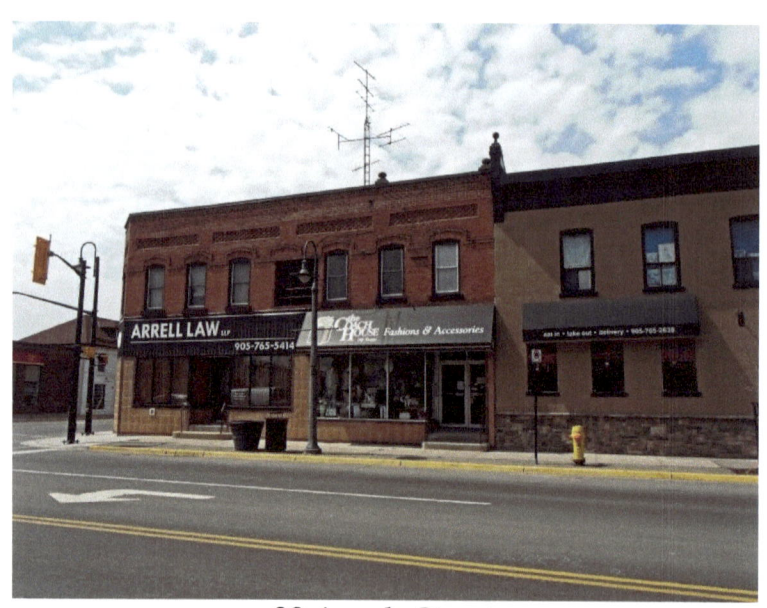

39 Argyle Street

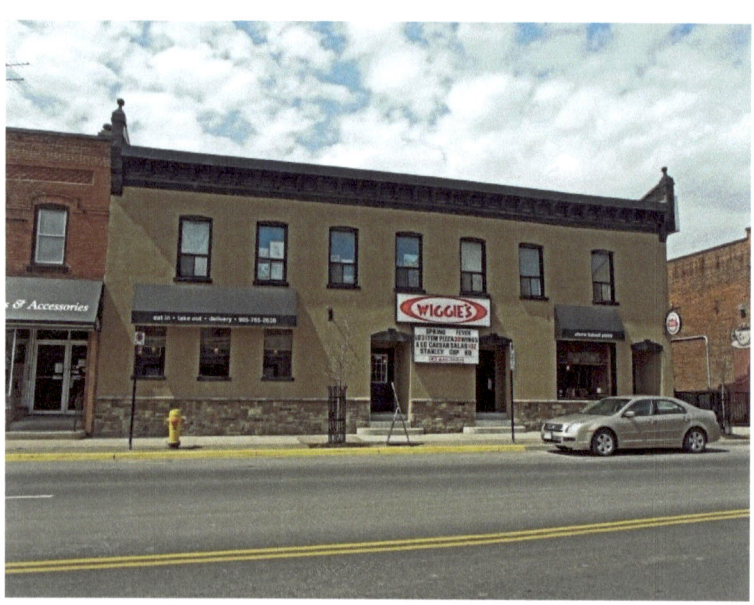

43 Argyle Street – Wiggie's Pizza

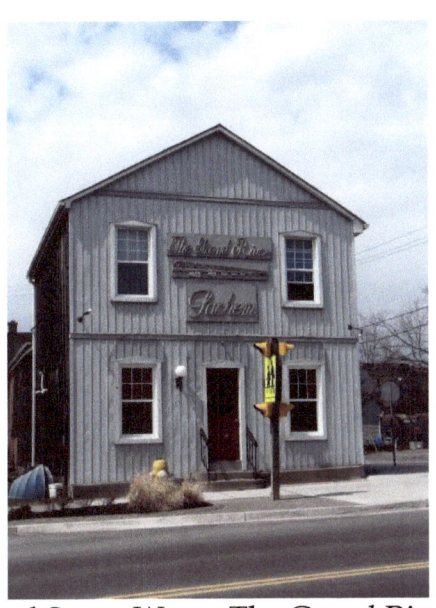

3 Sutherland Street West - The Grand River Sachem Newspaper Office – 1866 – One of Ontario's oldest weekly newspapers, the Sachem has published weekly from 1856. The founding publisher and owner of Sachem was Thomas Messenger.

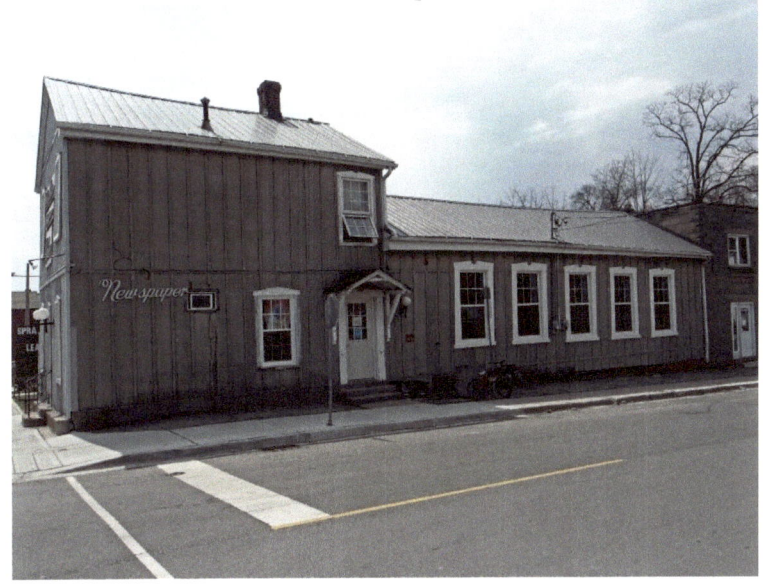

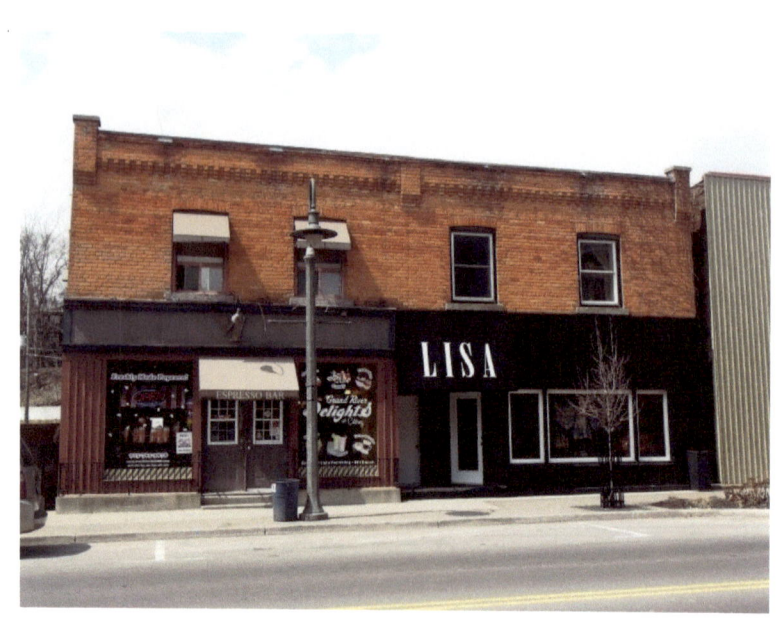

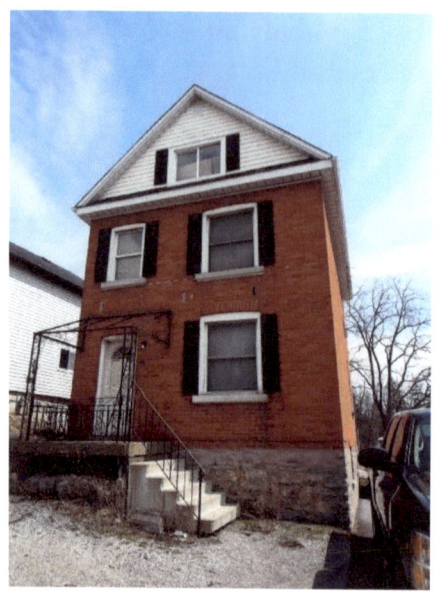

90 Argyle Street – Edwardian

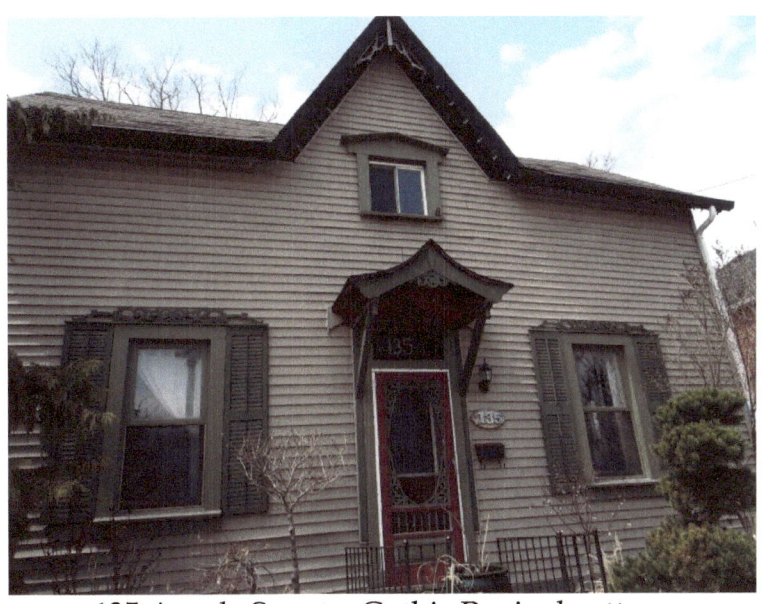

135 Argyle Street – Gothic Revival cottage

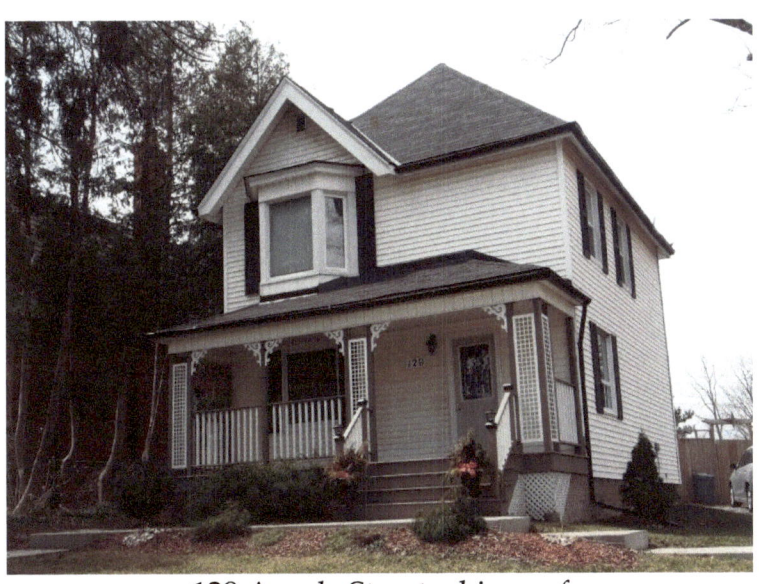

129 Argyle Street – hip roof

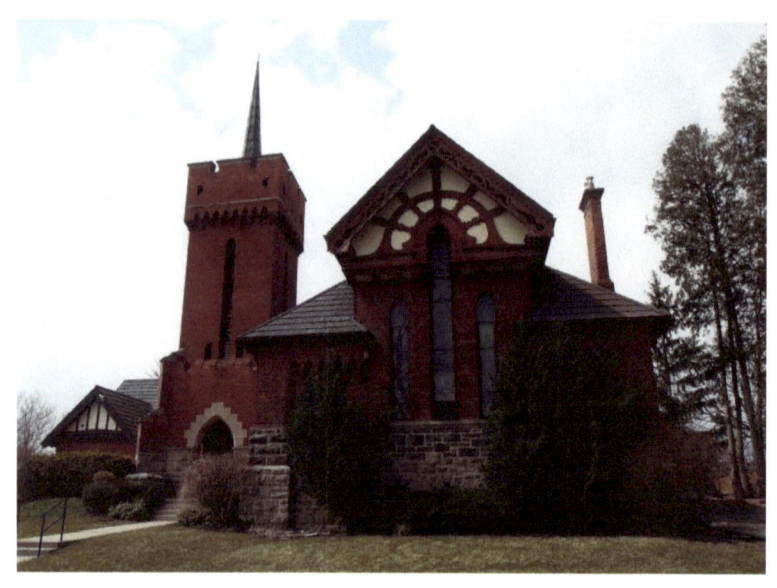

117 Argyle Street – Caledonia Presbyterian Church - 1898

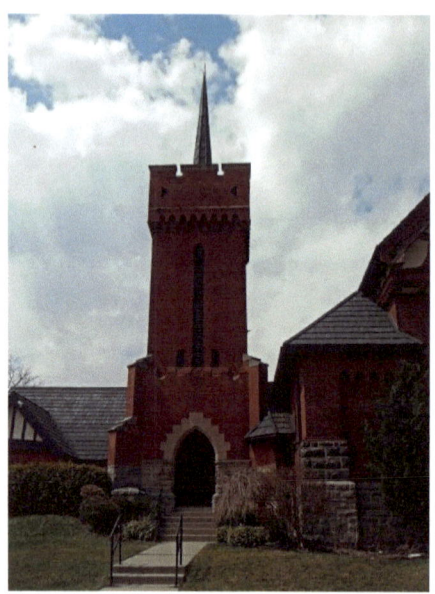

Battlemented tower with steeple

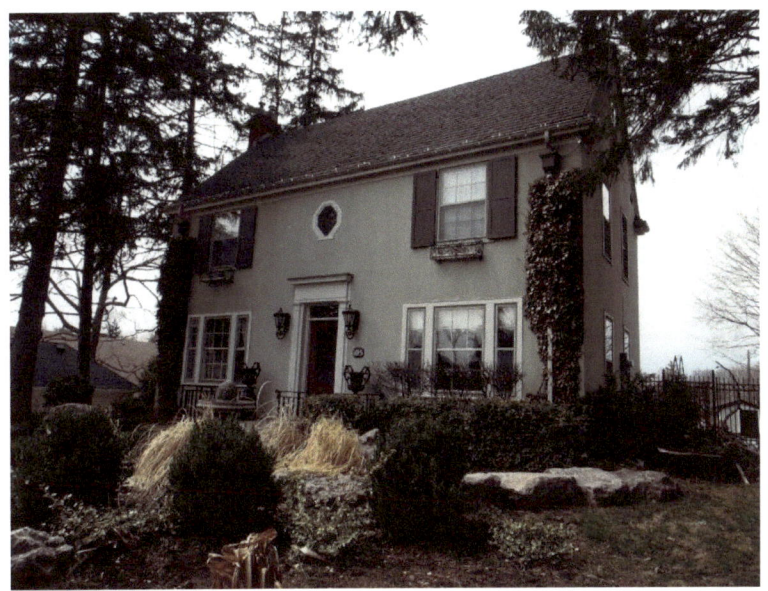

105 Argyle Street – Gothic Revival

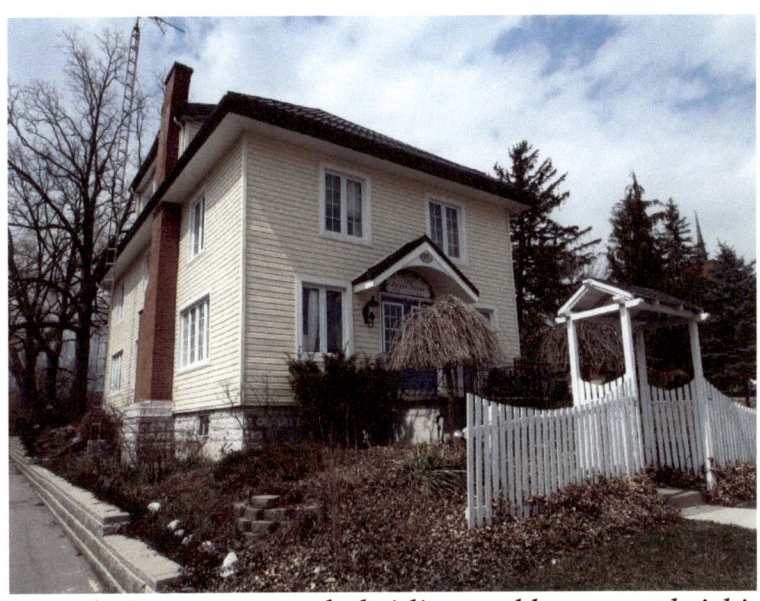

99 Argyle Street – upgraded siding and basement bricking

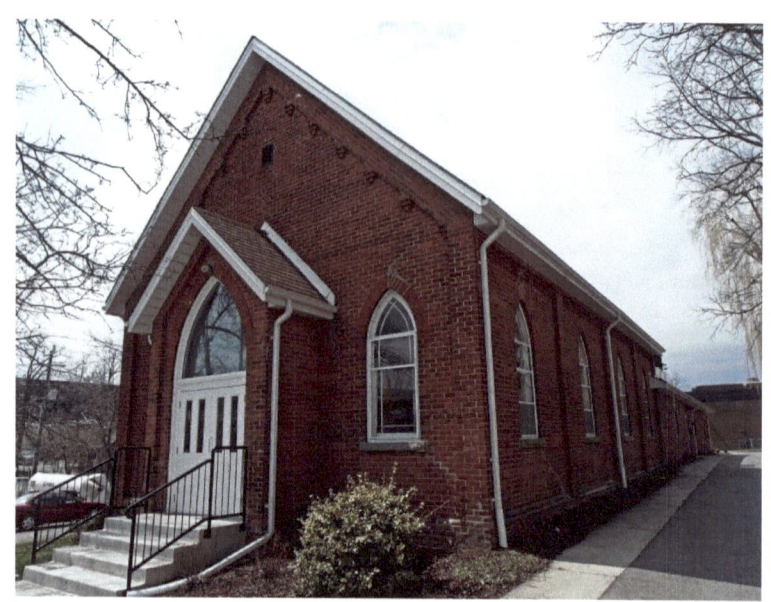

Caledonia Congregational Church – Argyle Street – Gothic – lancet windows

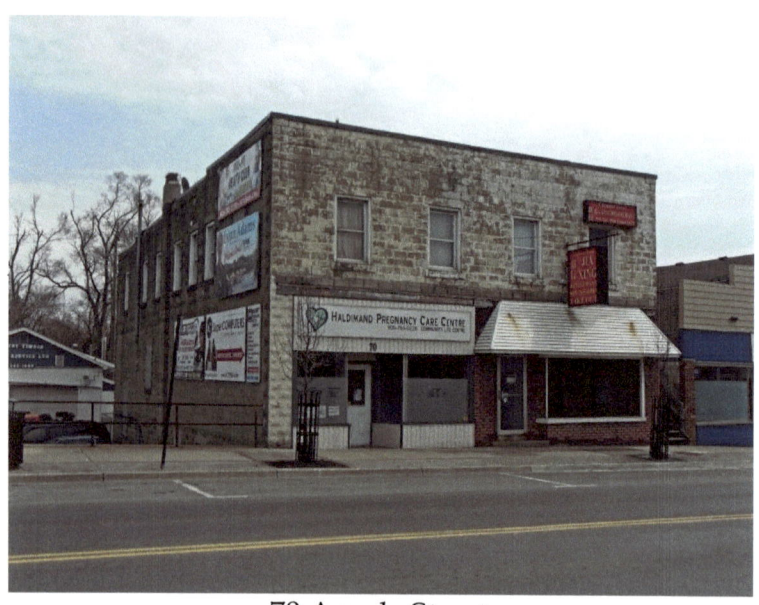

70 Argyle Street

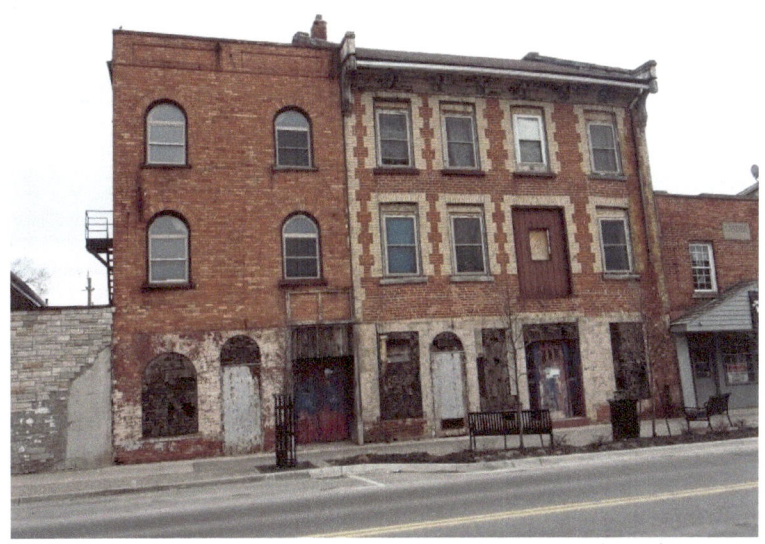

Dichromatic brickwork, paired cornice brackets

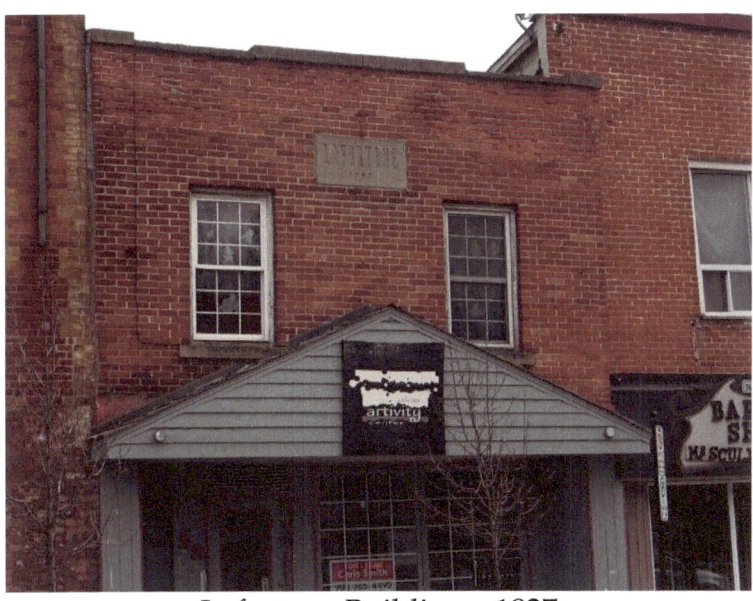

Lafortune Building – 1927

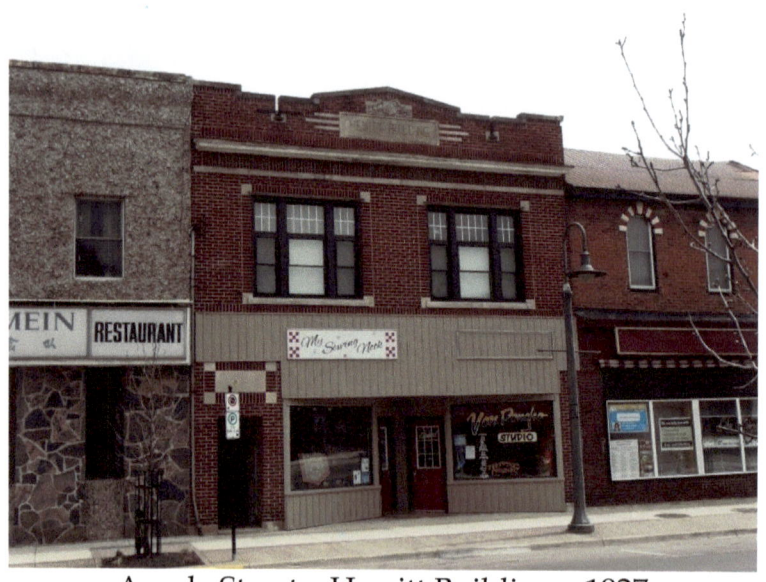

Argyle Street – Hewitt Building – 1927

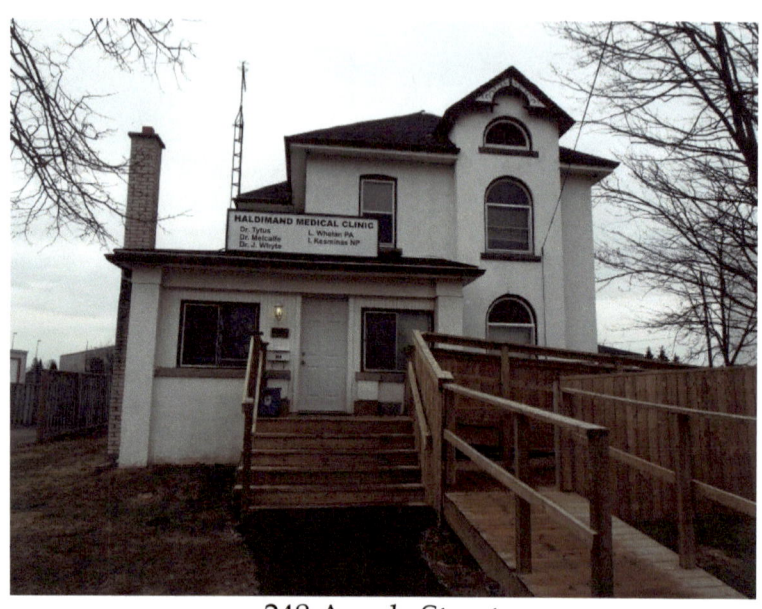

248 Argyle Street

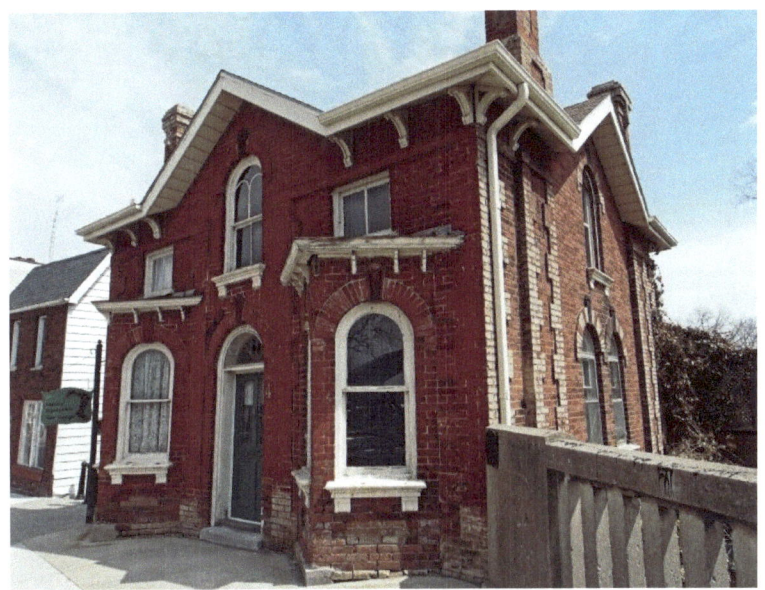

4 Argyle Street – Toll House c. 1875 – built as an office and residence for the collector of tolls for those crossing the bridge over the Grand River – Victorian architecture

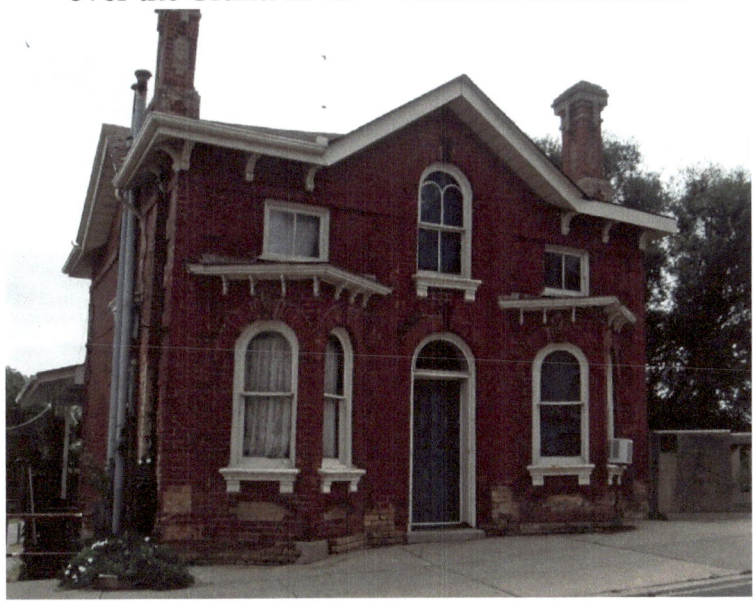

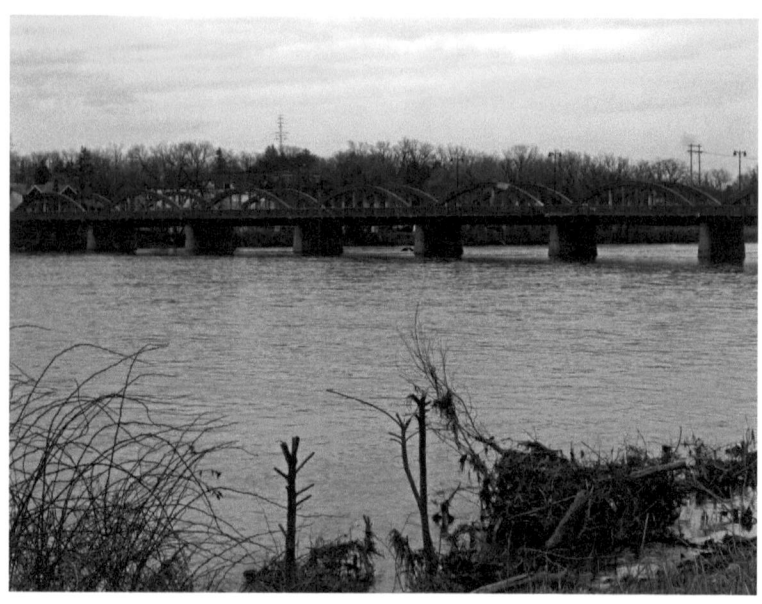

Caledonia Bridge – 1927 – Argyle Street – nine span reinforced concrete bridge

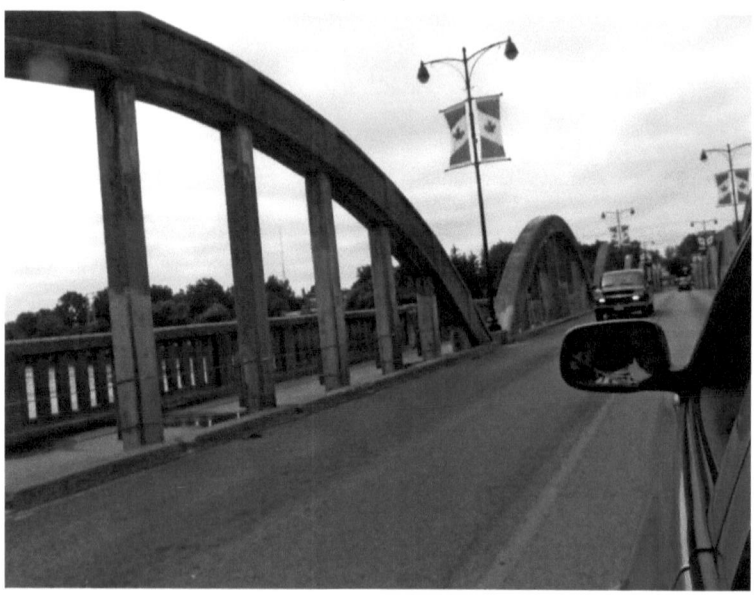

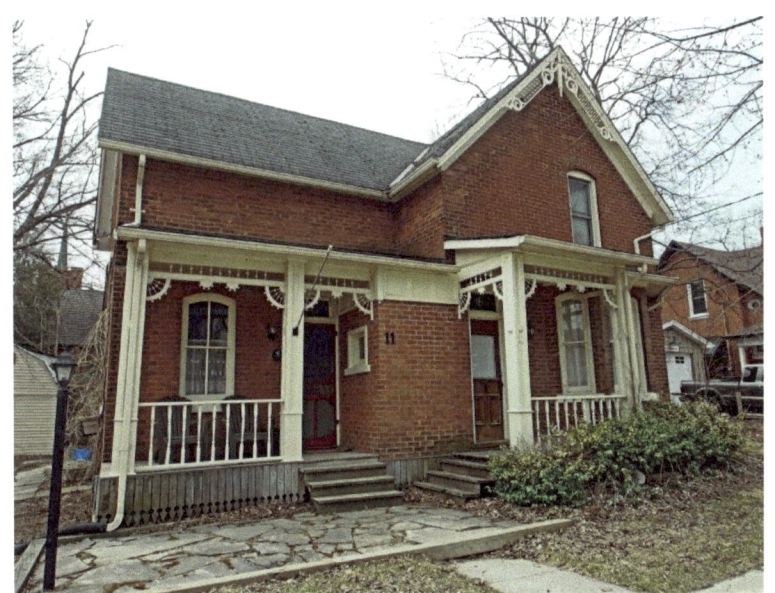

11 Orkney Street – Gothic Revival

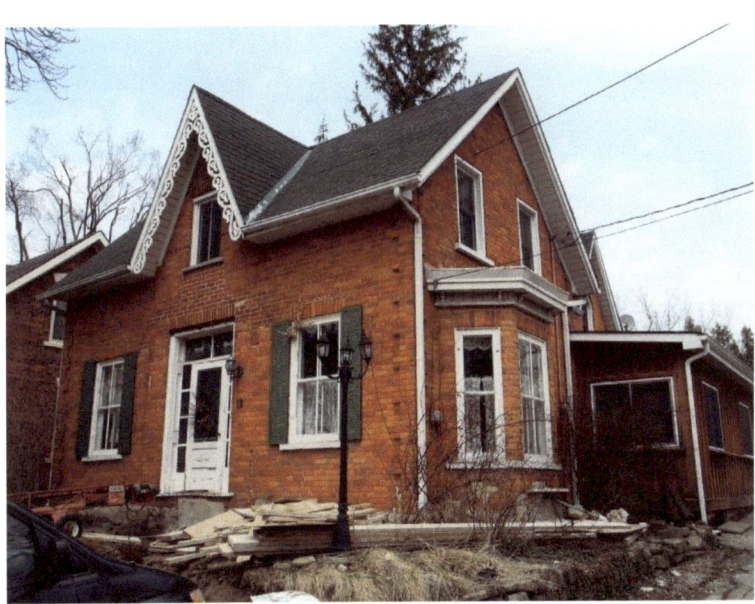

18 Orkney Street – Gothic Revival – verge board trim on gable, bay window on side

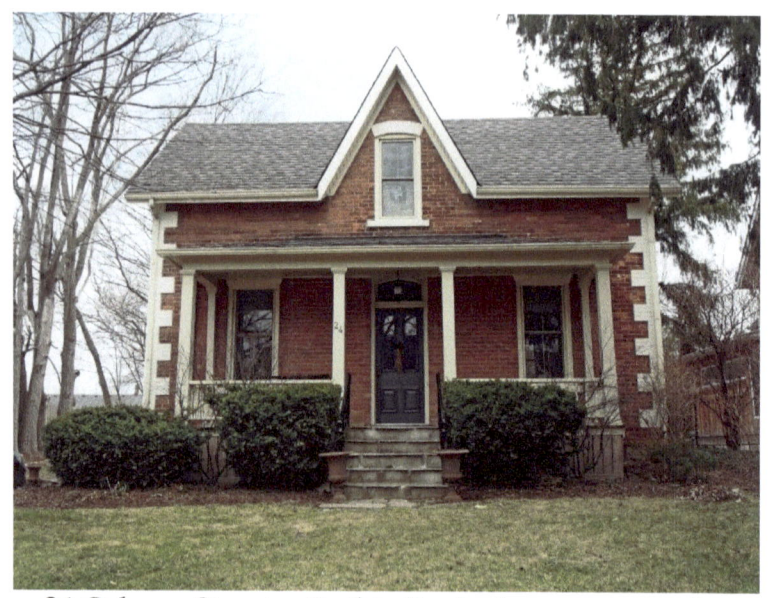

24 Orkney Street – Gothic Revival – corner quoins

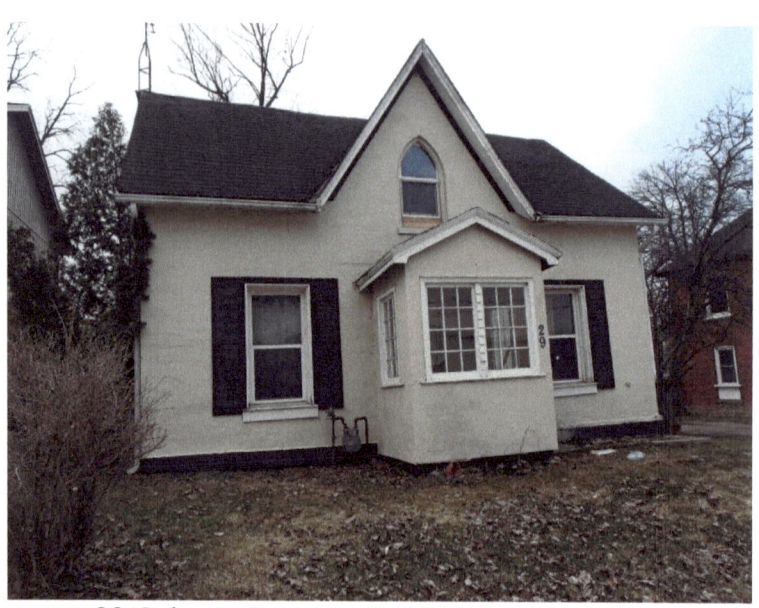

29 Orkney Street – Gothic Revival cottage

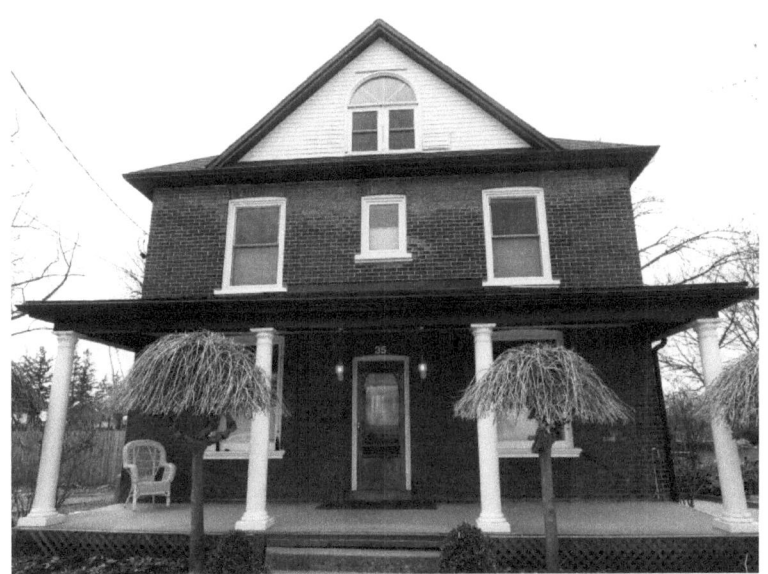

35 Orkney Street

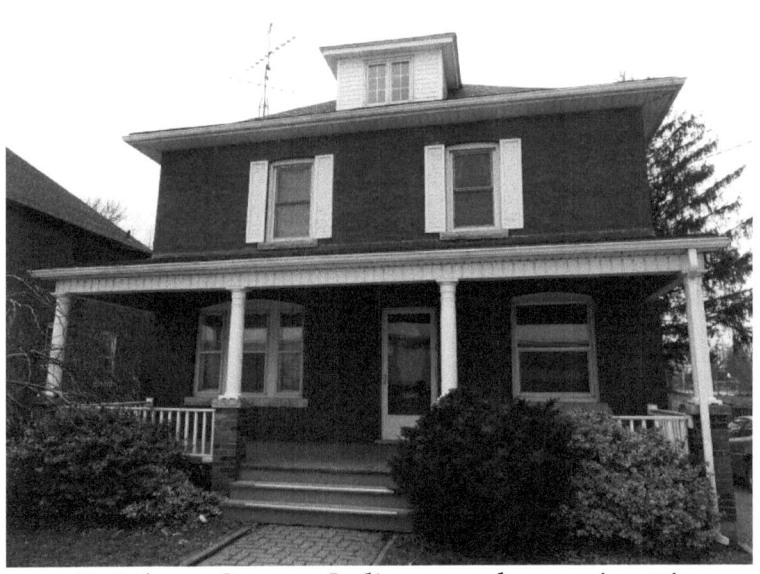

43 Orkney Street – Italianate – dormer in attic

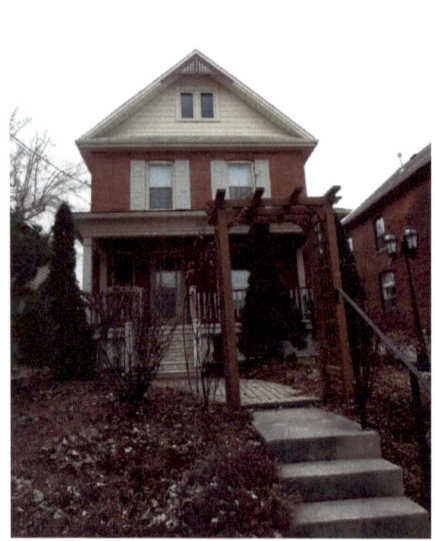
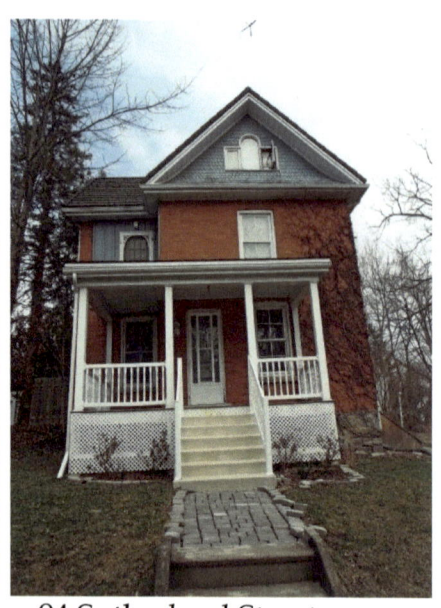

59 Orkney Street
Edwardian

94 Sutherland Street
Edwardian, Palladian window

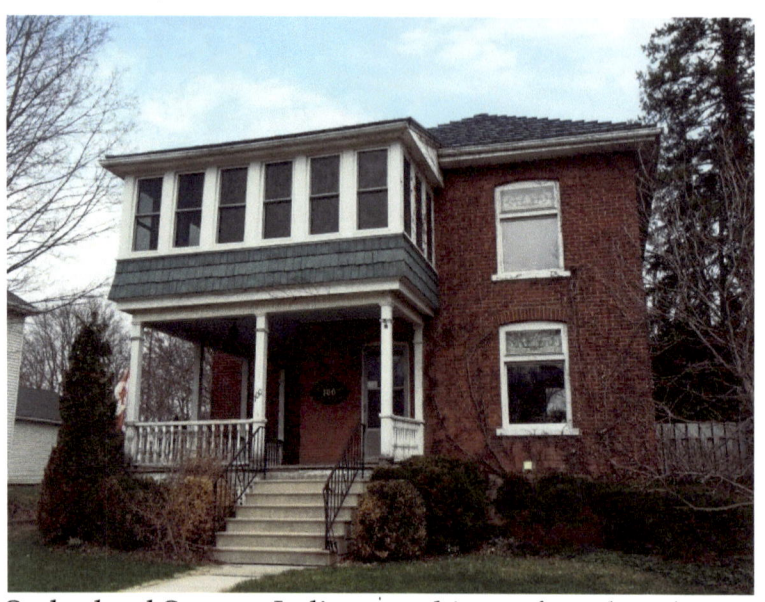

100 Sutherland Street – Italianate – hip roof, enclosed sunroom above verandah

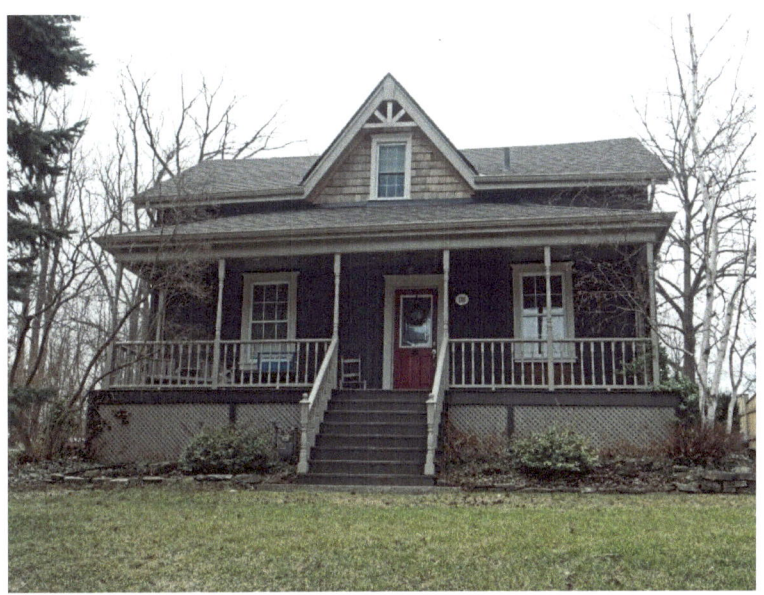

101 Sutherland Street – Gothic Revival cottage

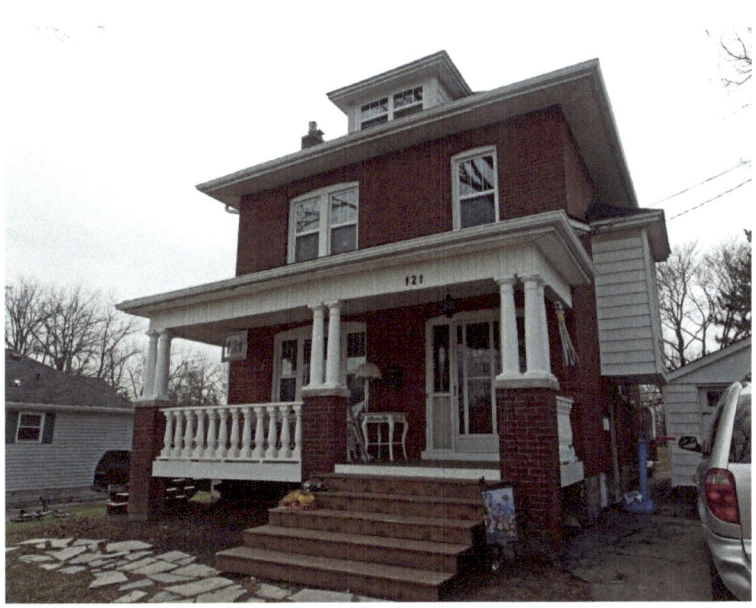

121 Sutherland Street – Italianate – dormer in attic

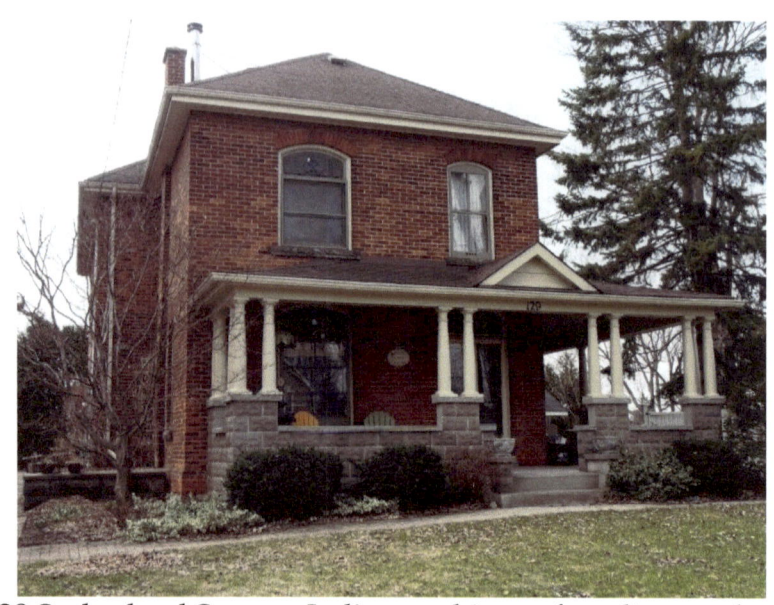

129 Sutherland Street – Italianate, hip roof, pediment above steps

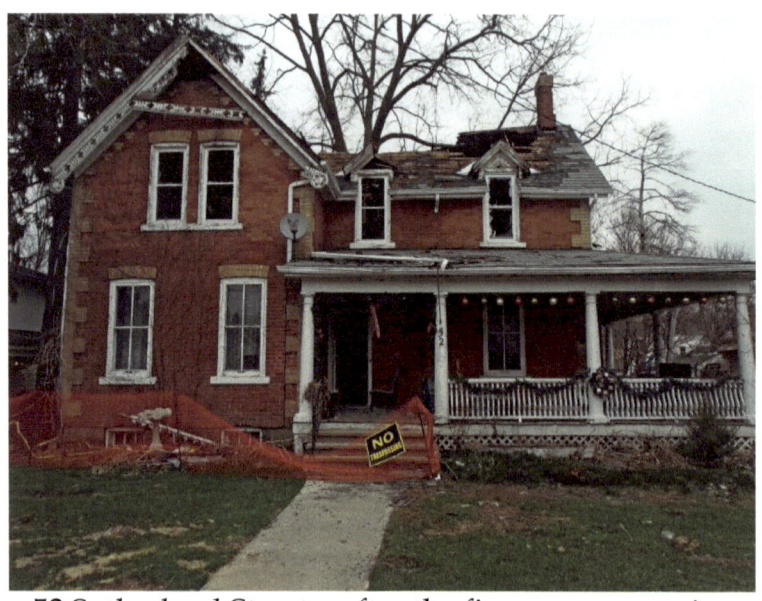

52 Sutherland Street – after the fire – corner quoins

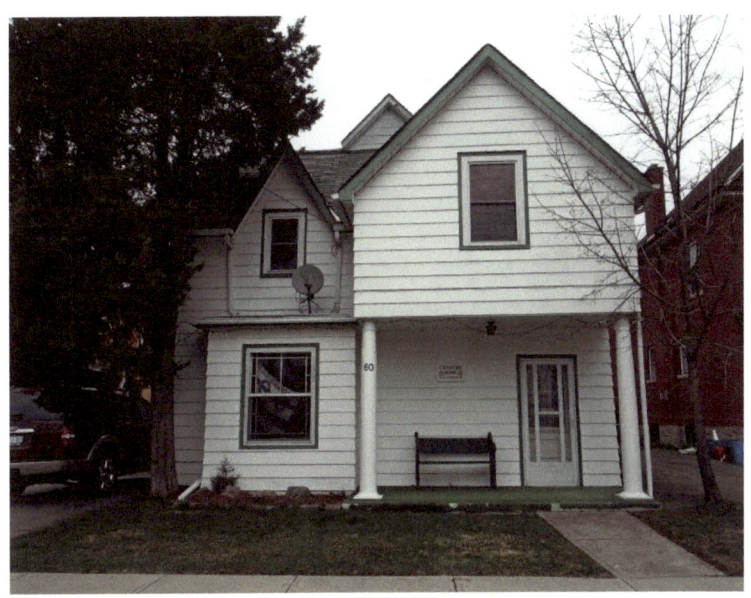

60 Sutherland Street - Gothic

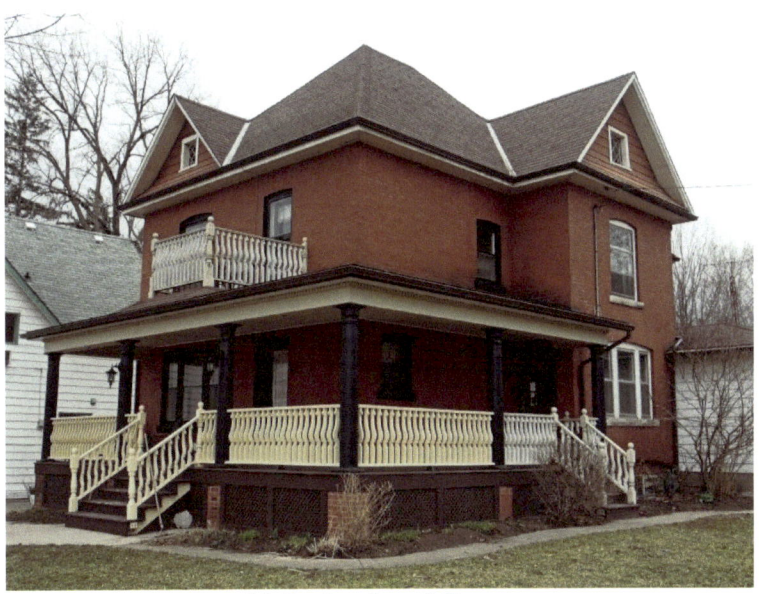

66 Sutherland Street

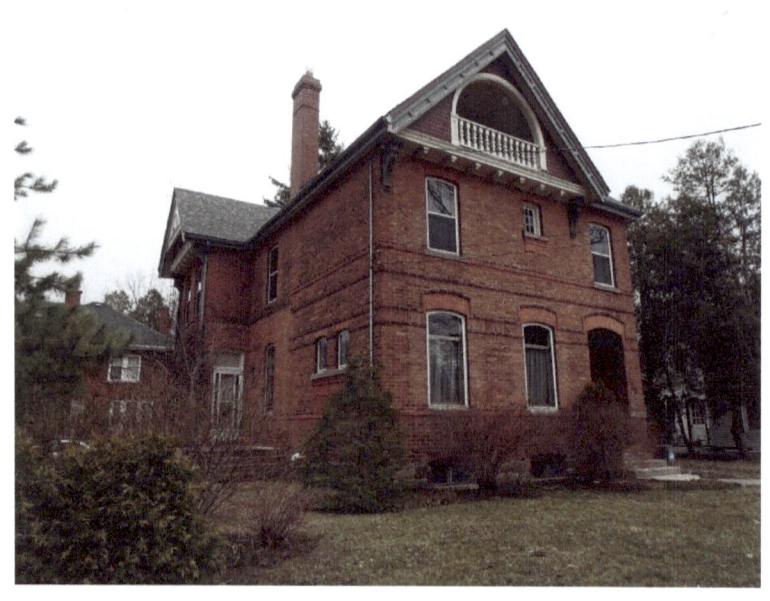

78 Sutherland Street

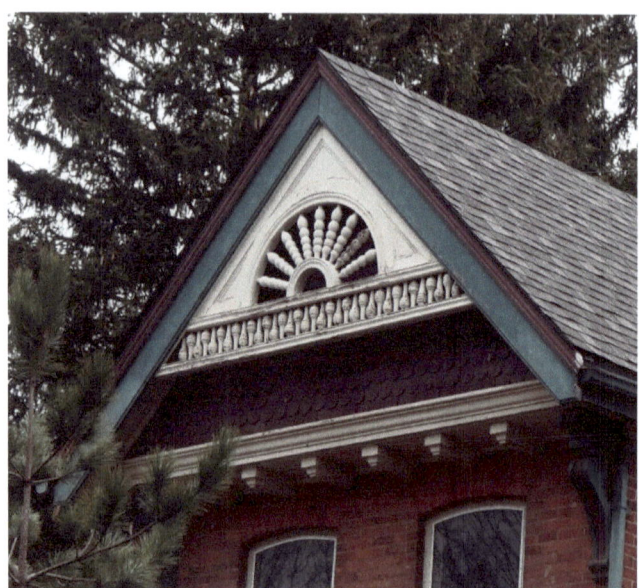

Gable detail

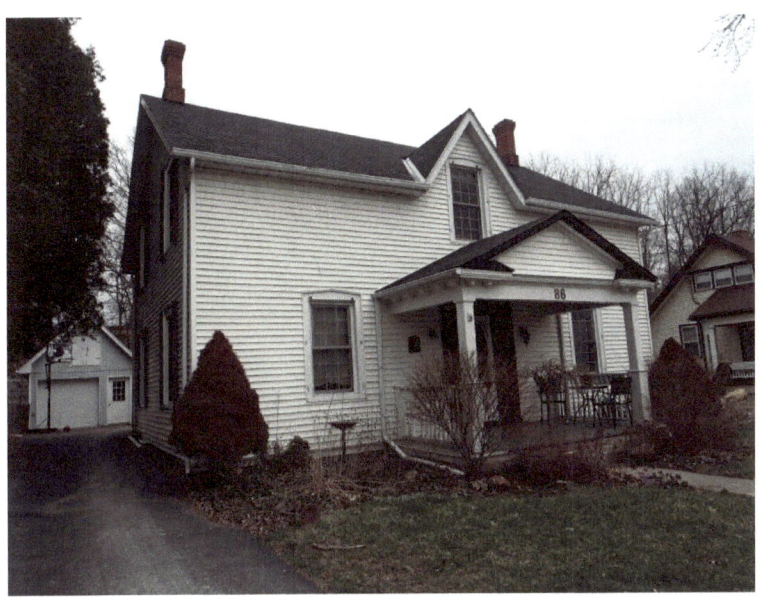

86 Sutherland Street - Gothic Revival

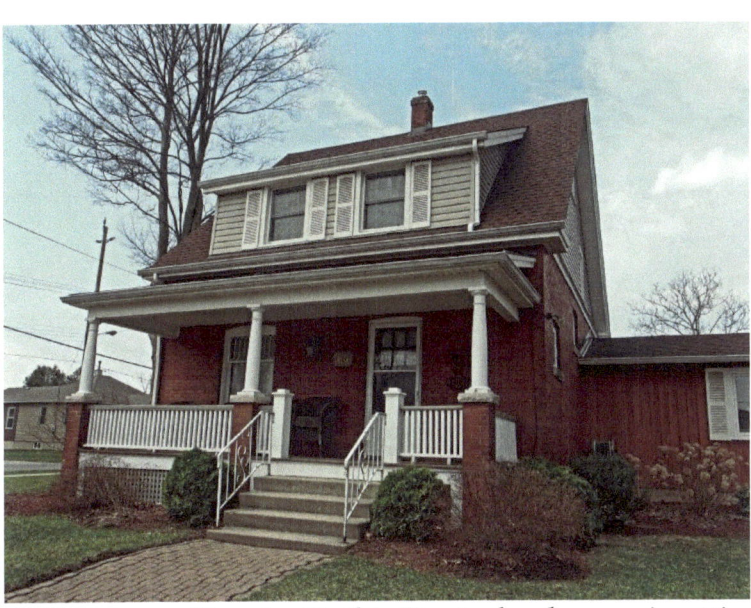

85 Inverness Street - Gothic Revival - dormer in attic

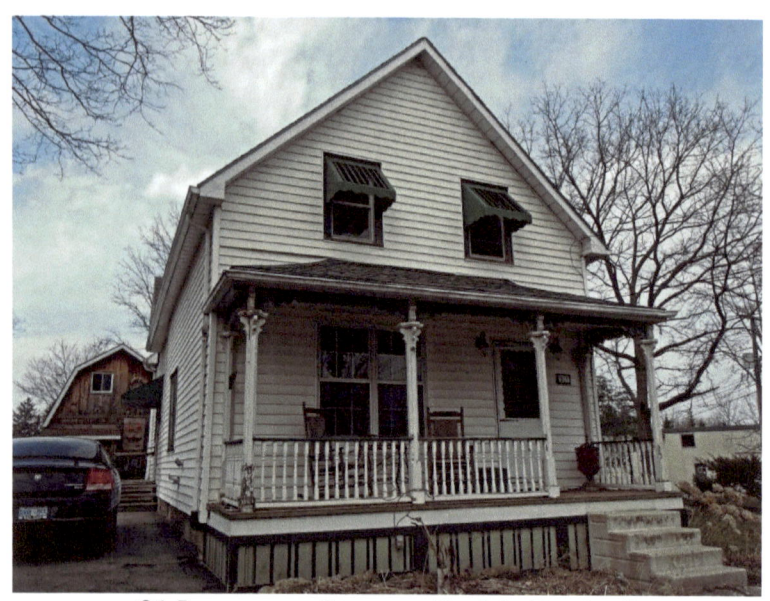

91 Inverness Street – Gothic Revival

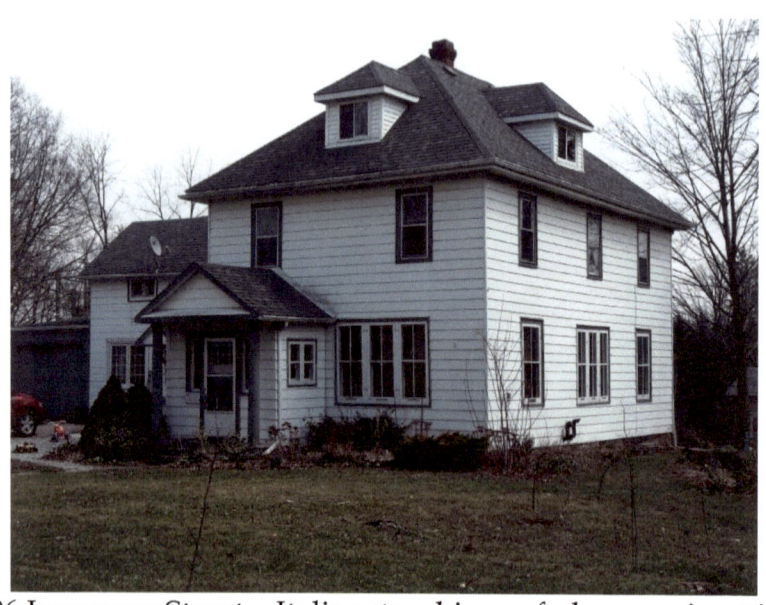

96 Inverness Street – Italianate – hip roof, dormers in attic

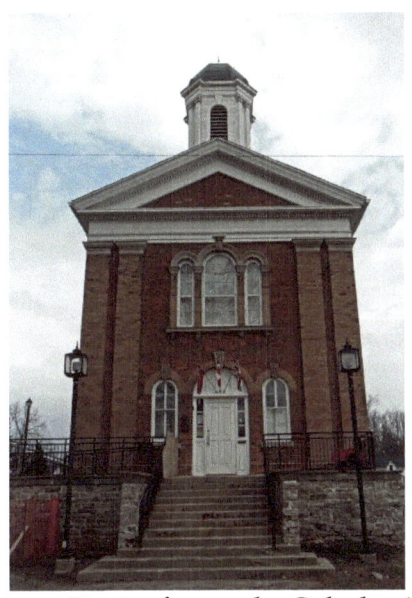

80 Caithness Street East – formerly Caledonia Town Hall – 1856 – Classical Georgian design - Pediment above front entrance, pilasters, dentil moulding below cornice

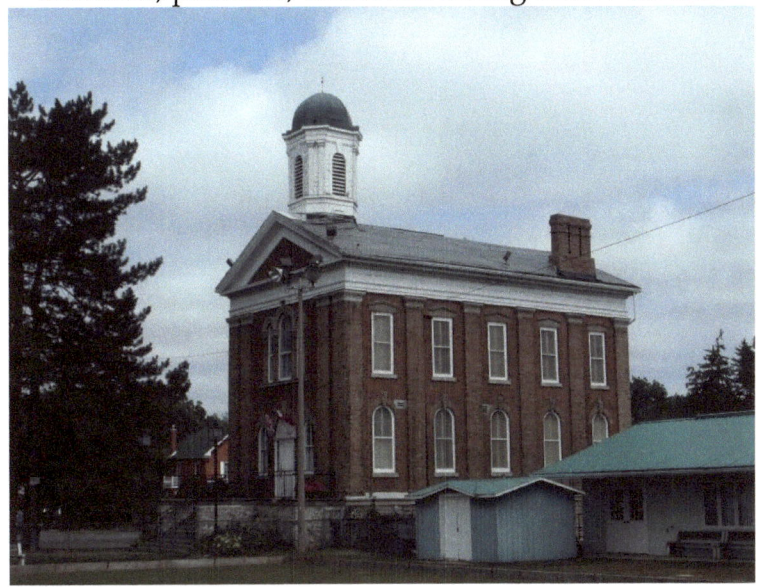

Cupola on roof, arched window voussoirs and keystones

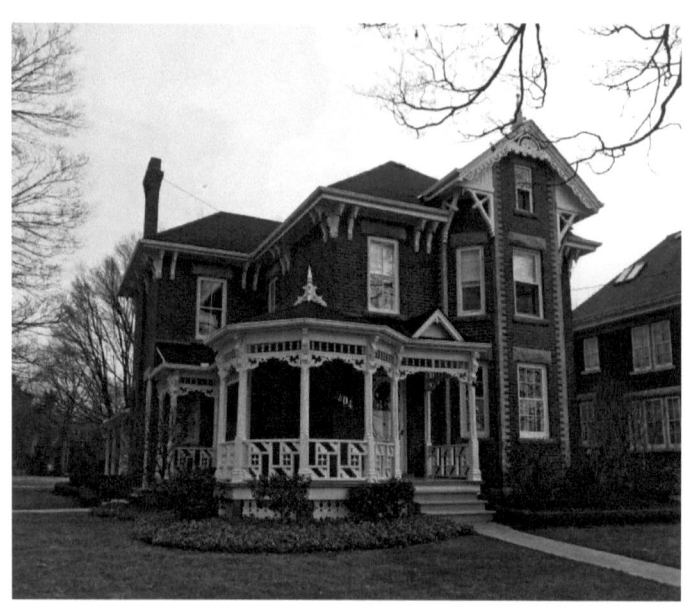

204 Caithness Street – paired cornice brackets

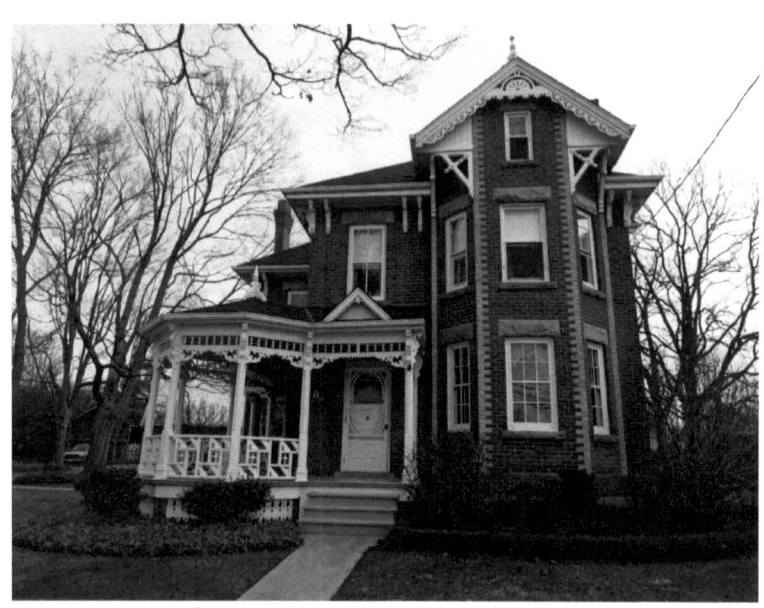

Corner quoins, decorative verge board trim on gable of two-and-a-half-storey tower-like bay

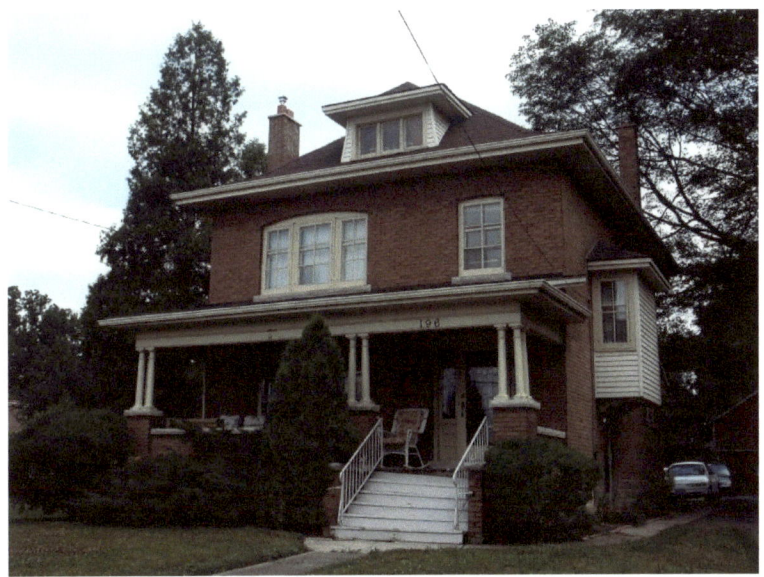

196 Caithness Street – Italianate style with dormer in attic

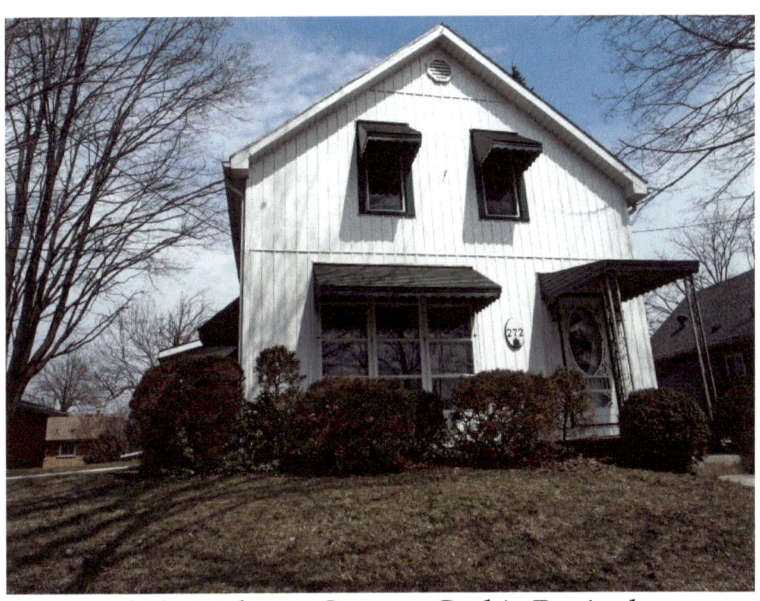

272 Caithness Street – Gothic Revival

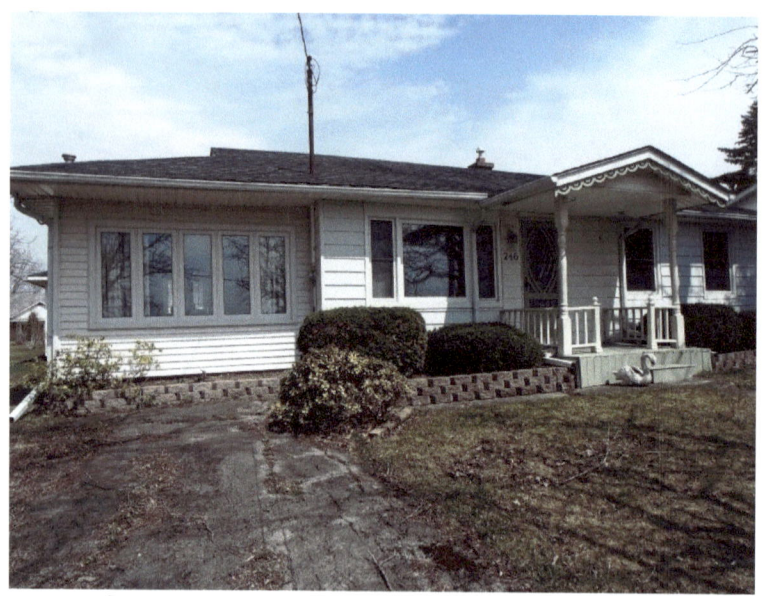

246 Caithness Street – one storey cottage

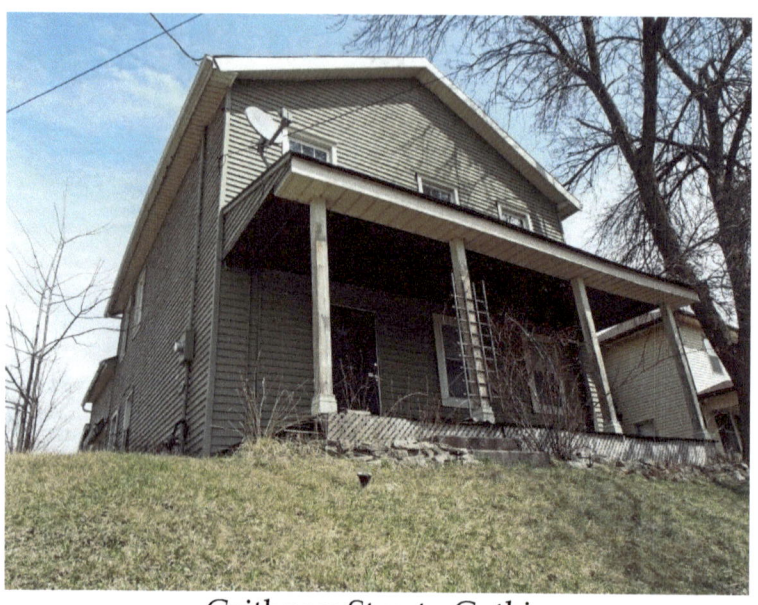

Caithness Street - Gothic

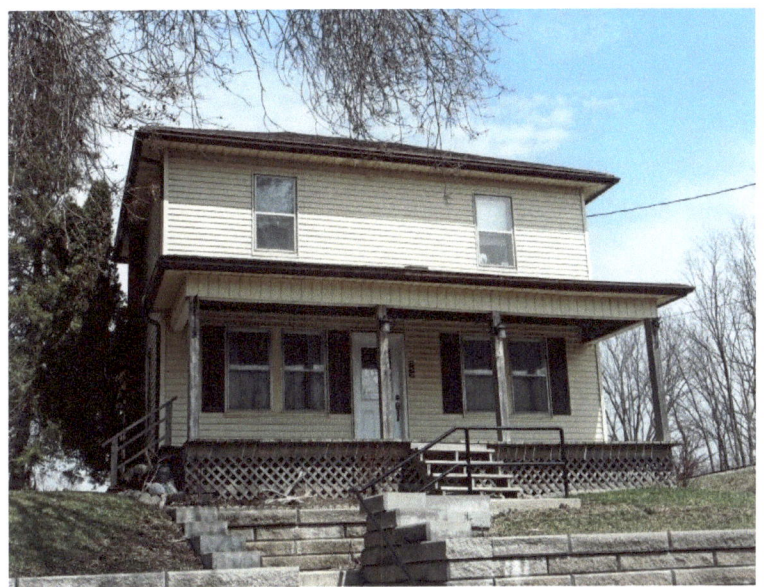

226 Caithness Street - Italianate

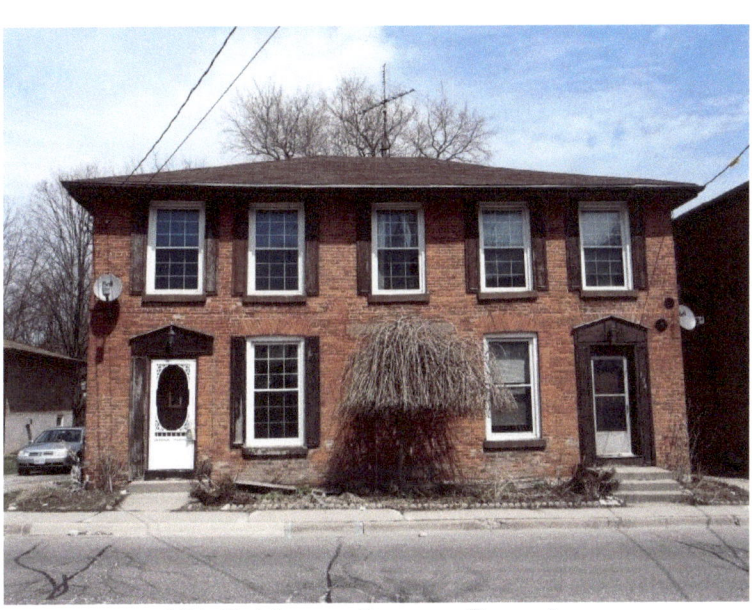

194 Caithness Street - Georgian

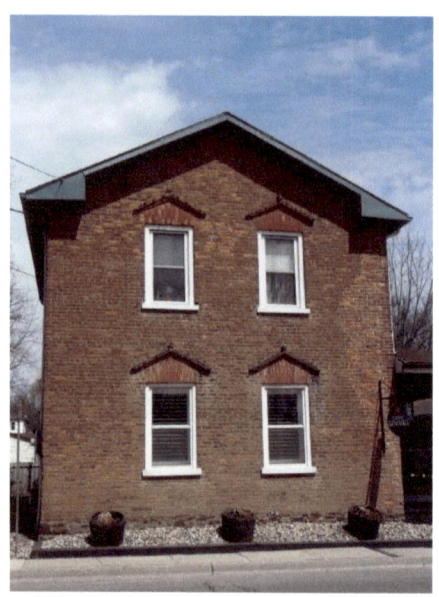

192 Caithness Street

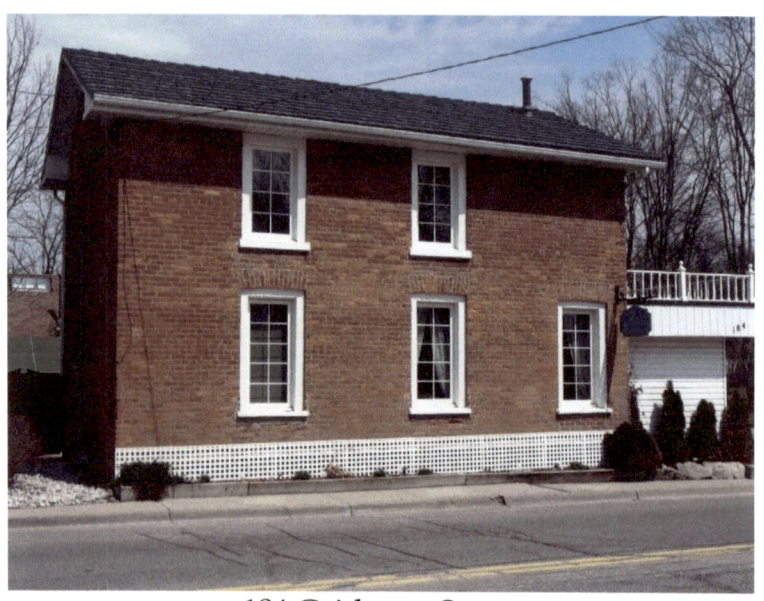

184 Caithness Street

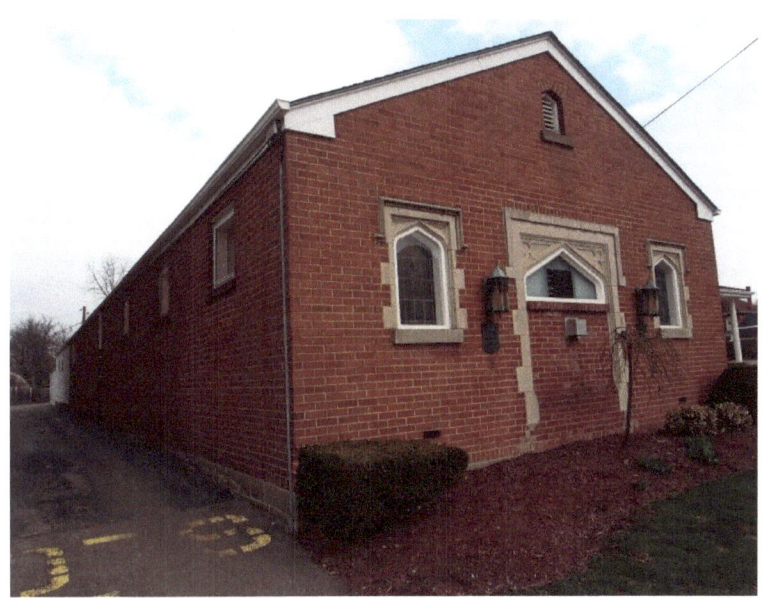

28 Caithness Street – Miller Funeral Chapel

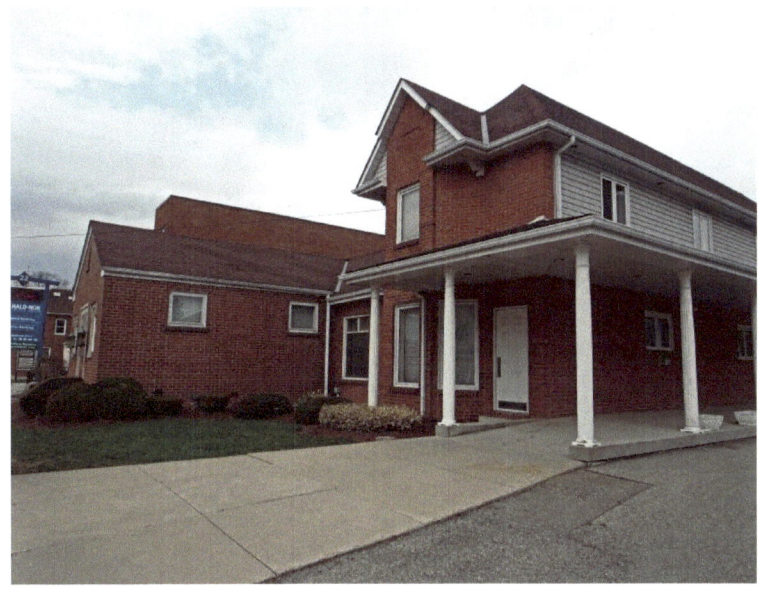

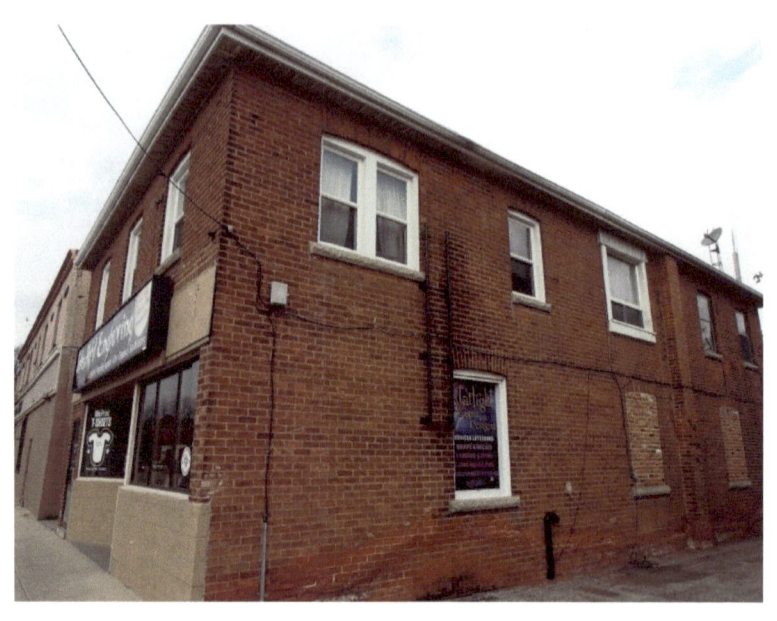

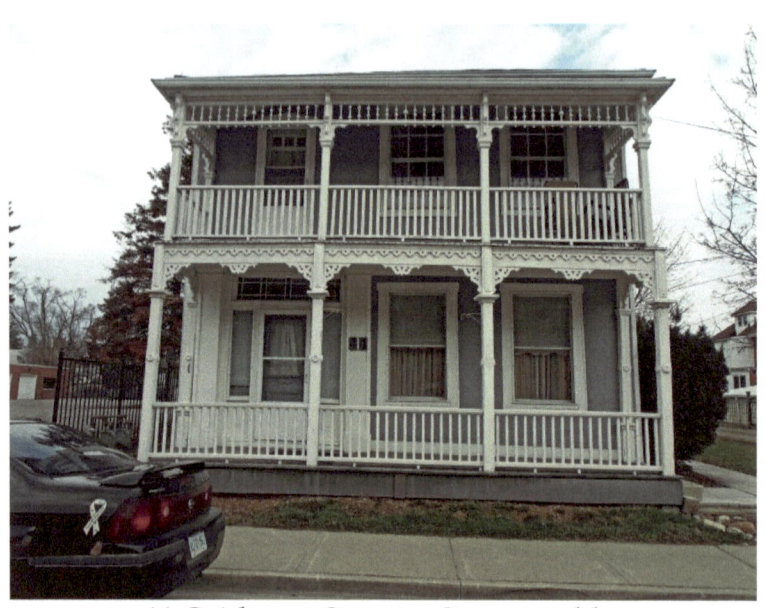

44 Caithness Street – Georgian-like

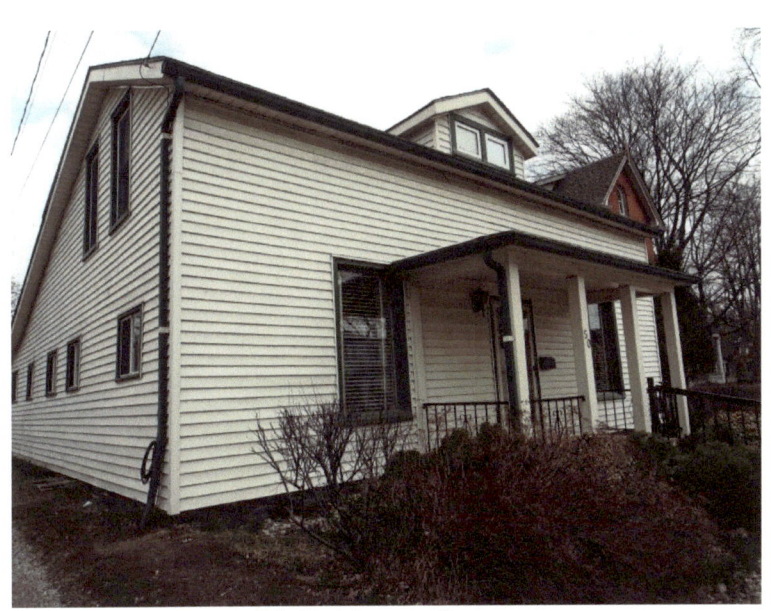

50 Caithness Street

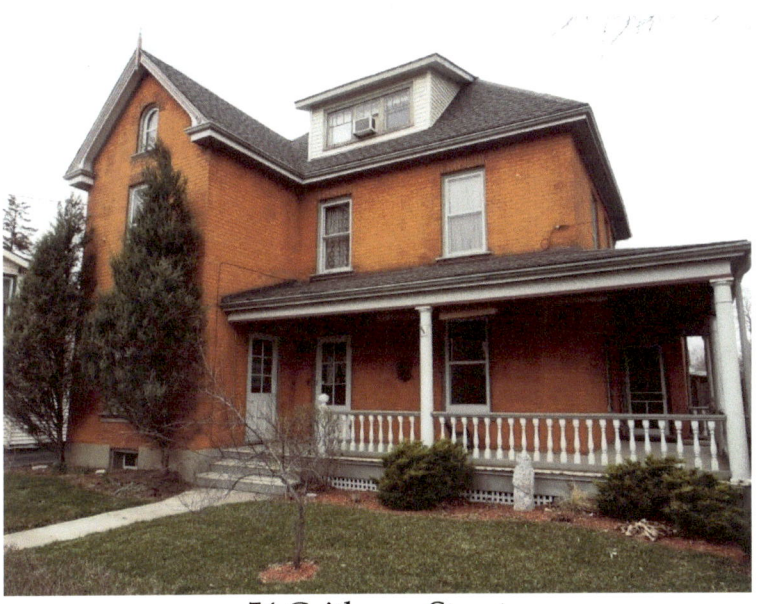

54 Caithness Street

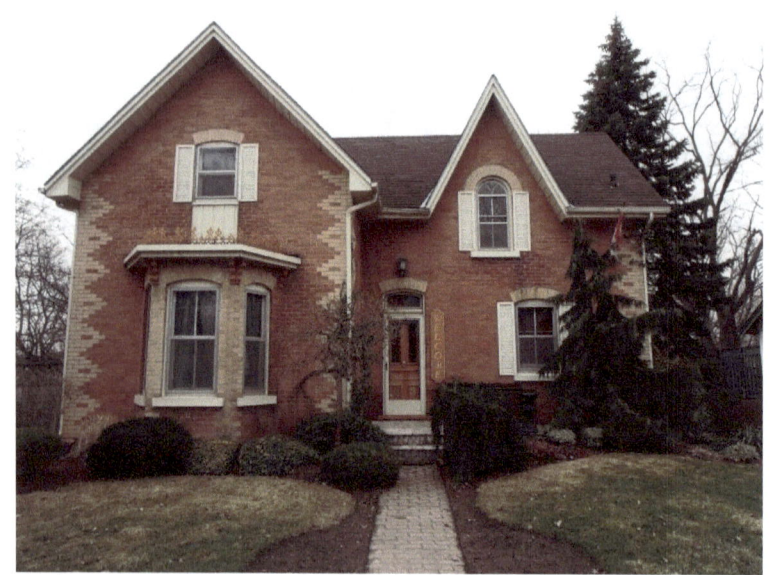

Caithness Street – Gothic Revival, dichromatic brickwork

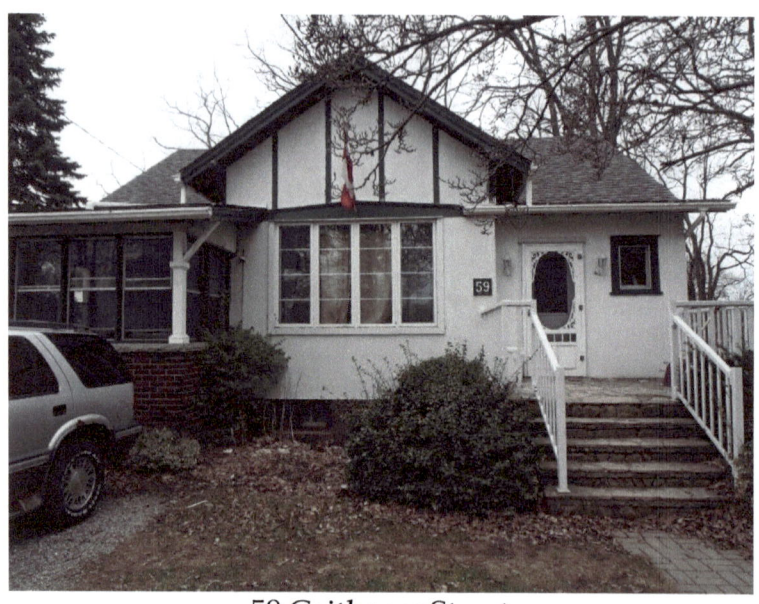

59 Caithness Street

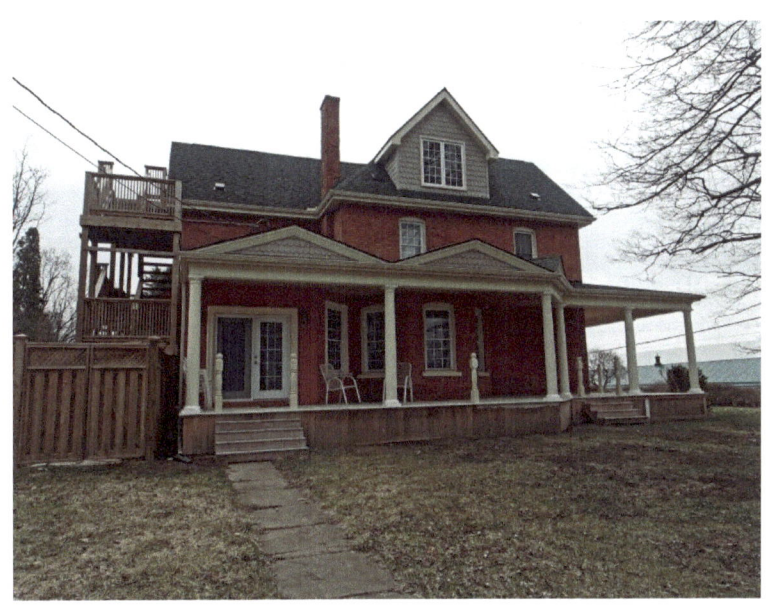

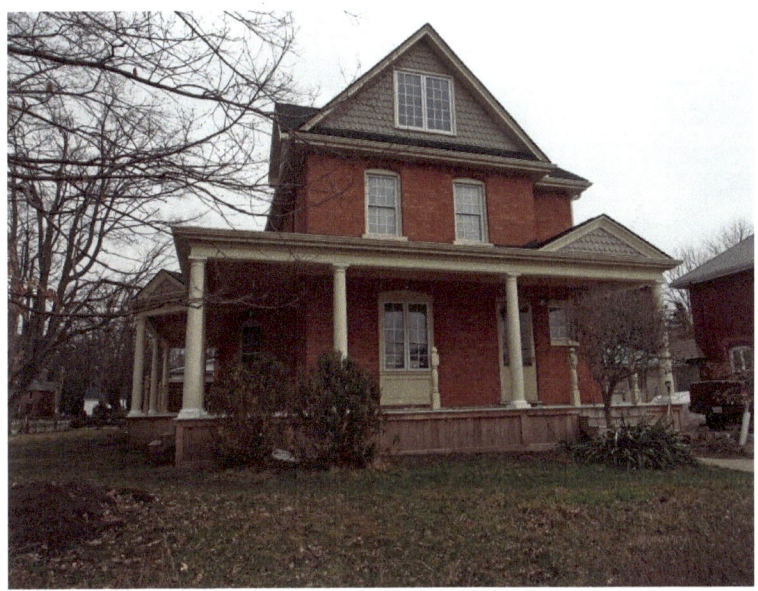

Edwardian style

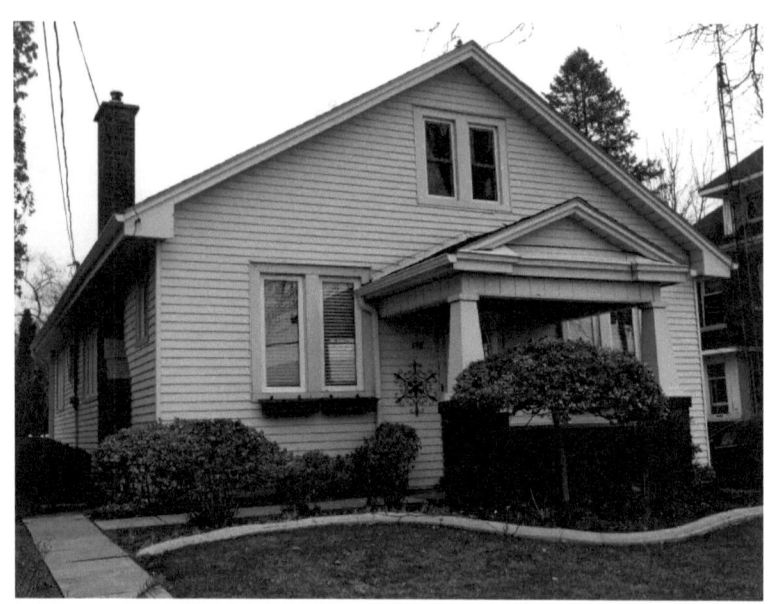

110 Caithness Street

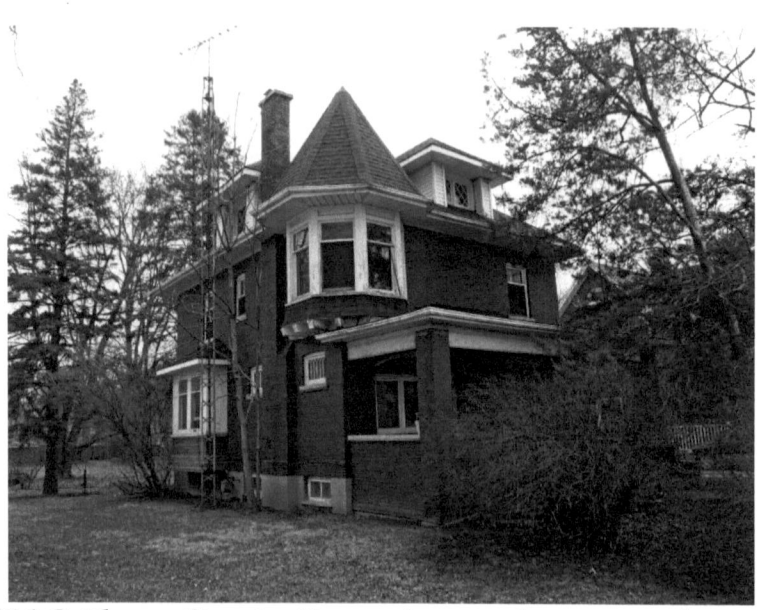

116 Caithness Street – Queen Anne style – turret, dormer

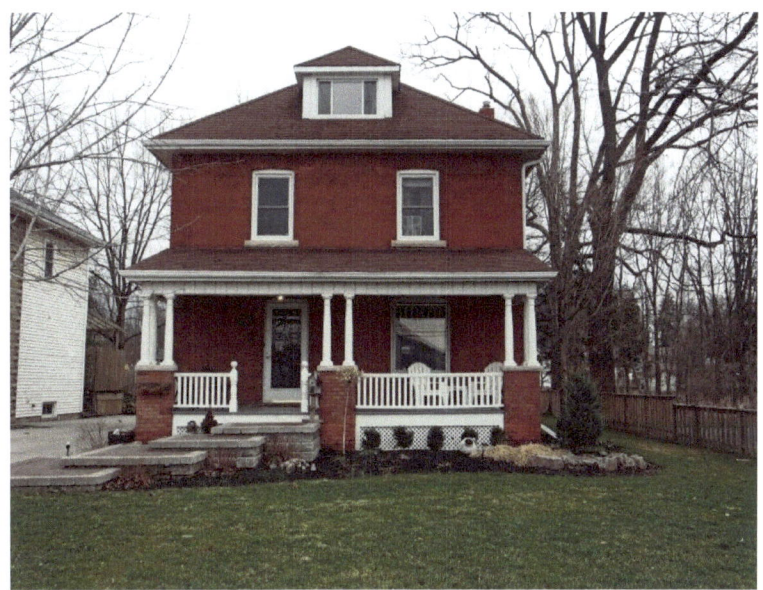

130 Caithness Street – Italianate – dormer in attic

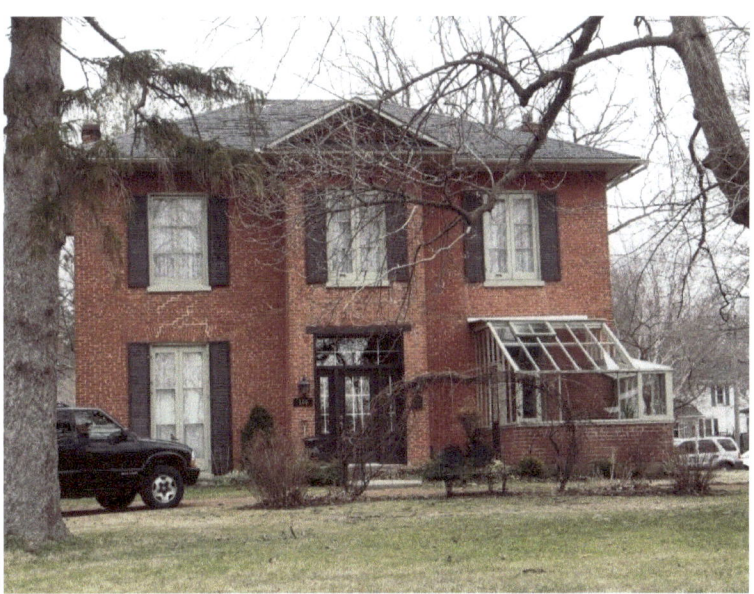

156 Caithness Street – McKinnon Smith house – The brick house was built in 1850 by Neil McKinnon, raised by Ranald McKinnon who was the founder of Caledonia.

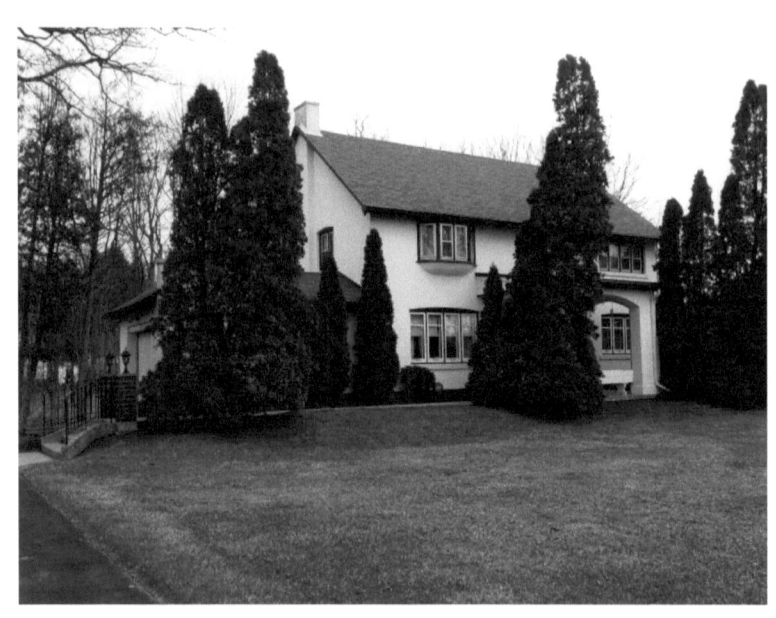

138 Caithness Street – Gothic Revival

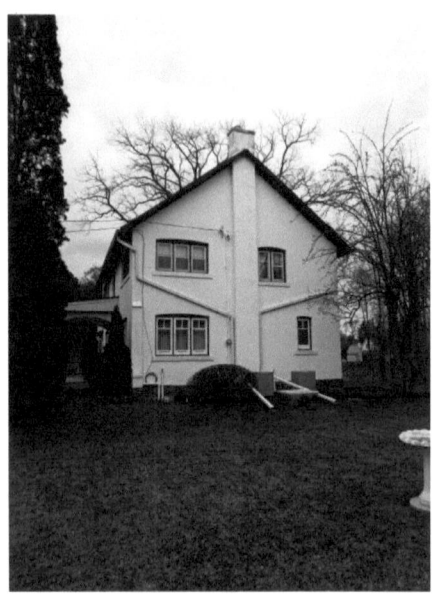

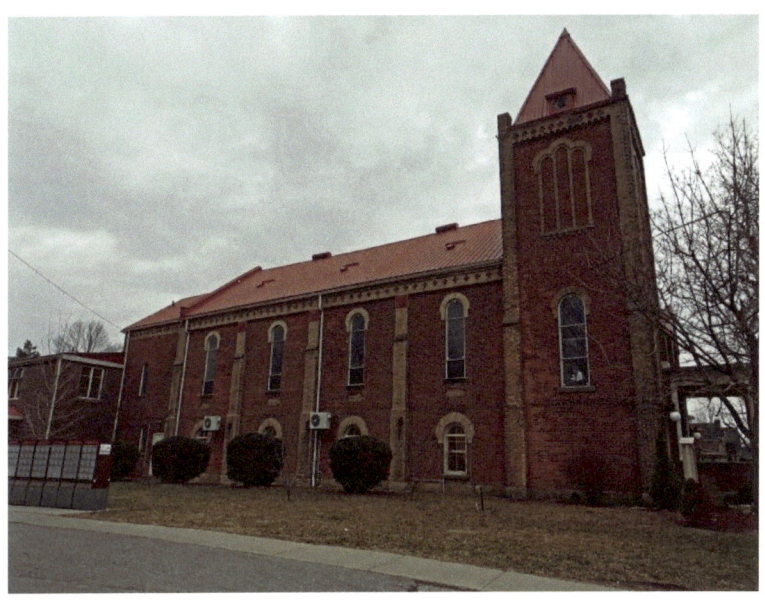

174 Caithness Street East – Grace United Church - buttresses, lancet windows, decorative brickwork

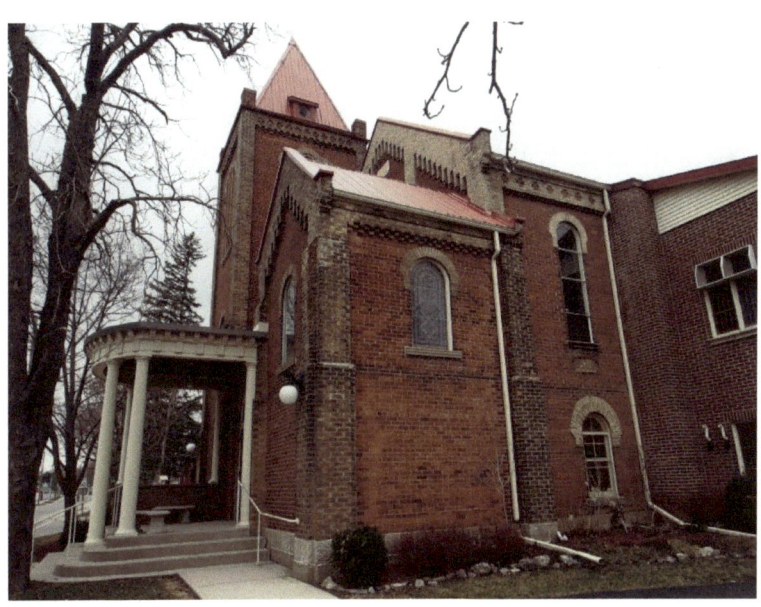

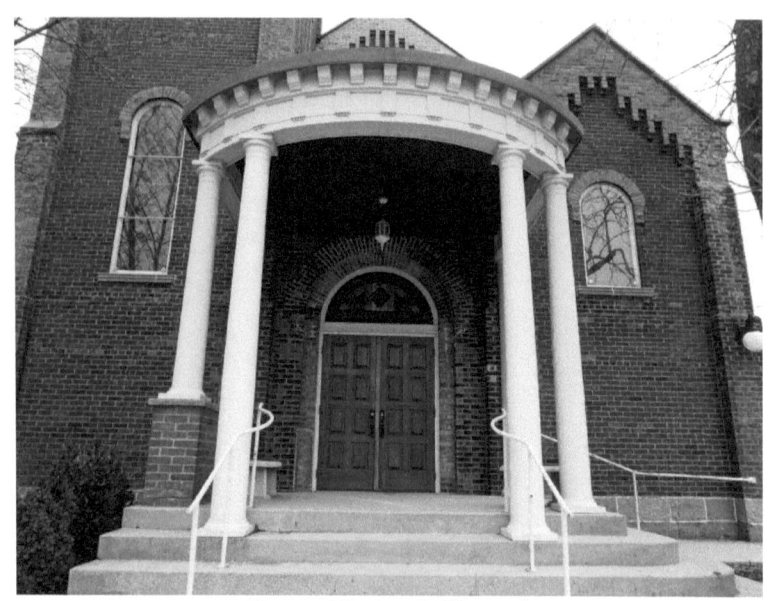

Grace United Church

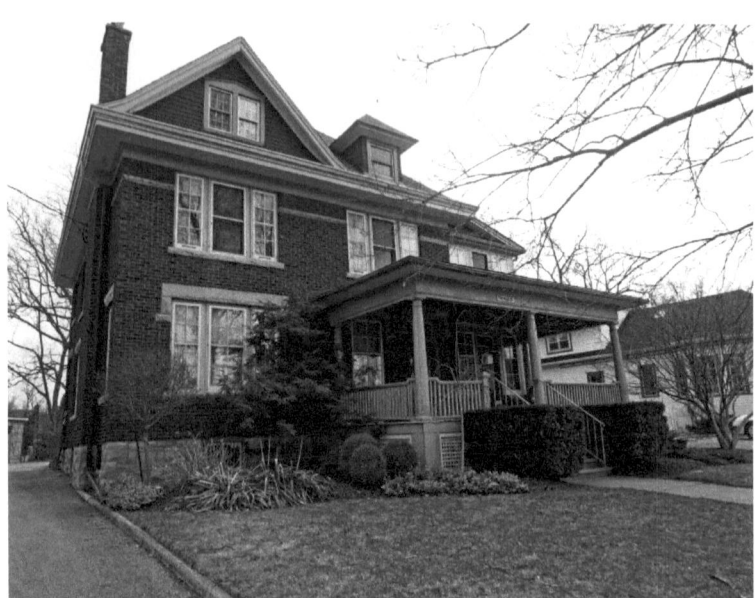

212 Caithness Street – Edwardian – dormer in attic

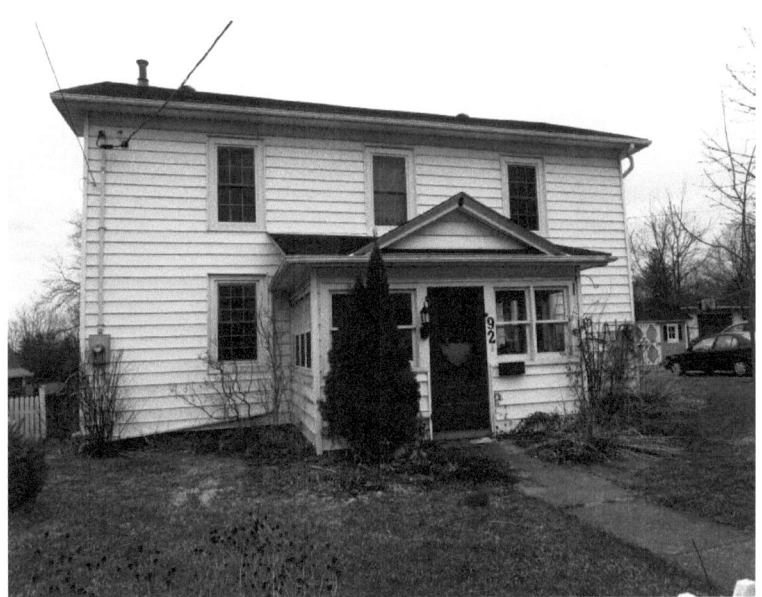

92 Caithness Street

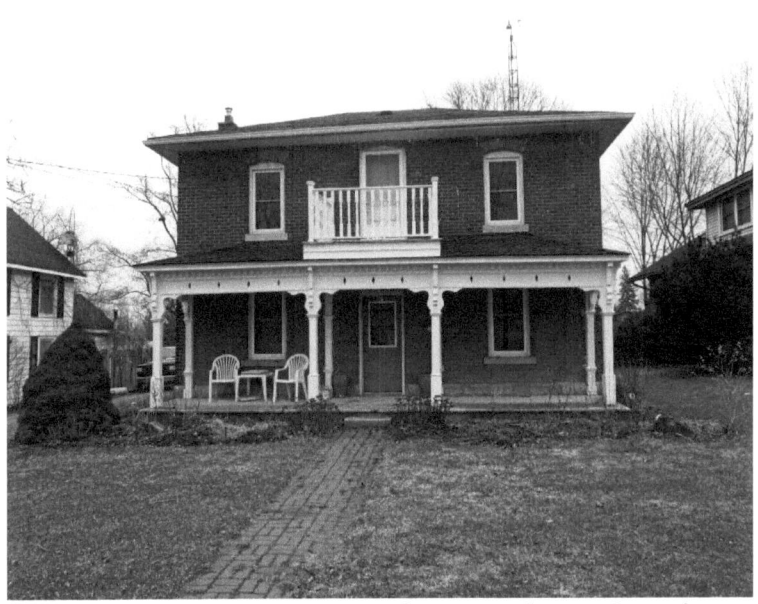

78 Caithness Street – Italianate – hipped roof

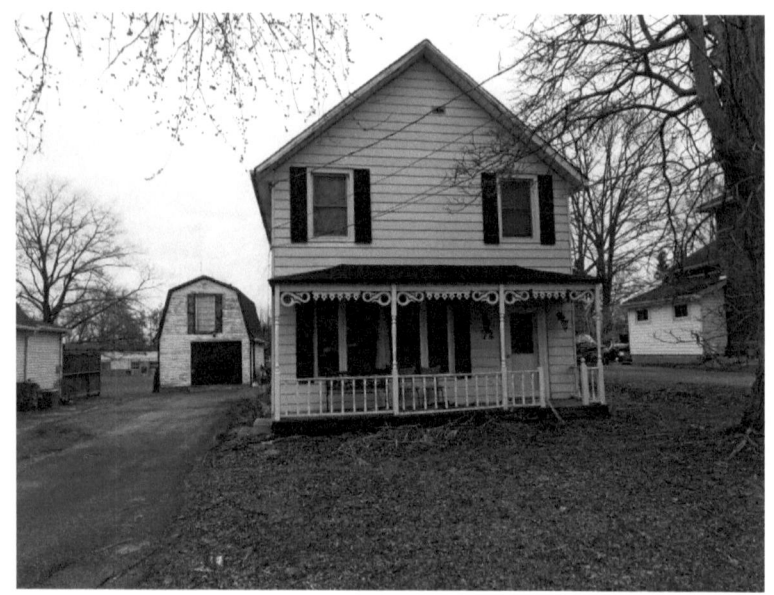

72 Caithness Street

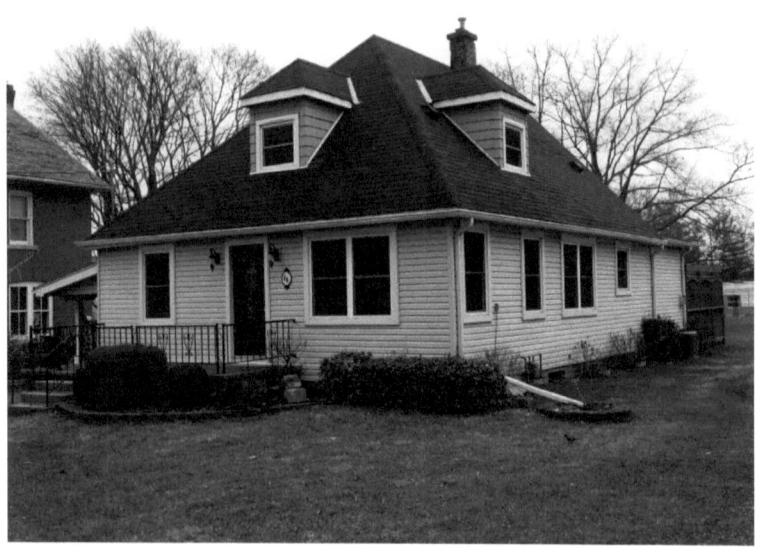

66 Caithness Street – steeply pitched hipped roof, dormers

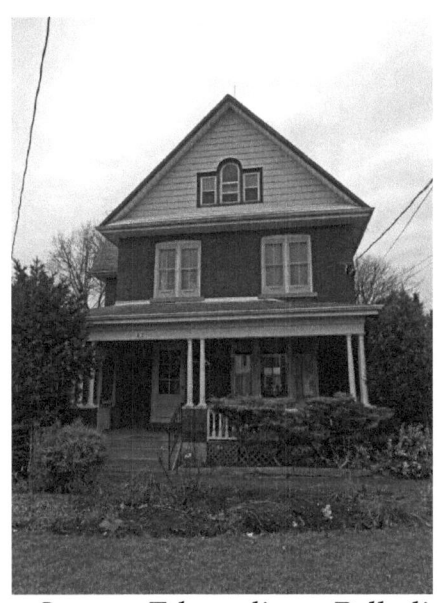

62 Caithness Street – Edwardian – Palladian window

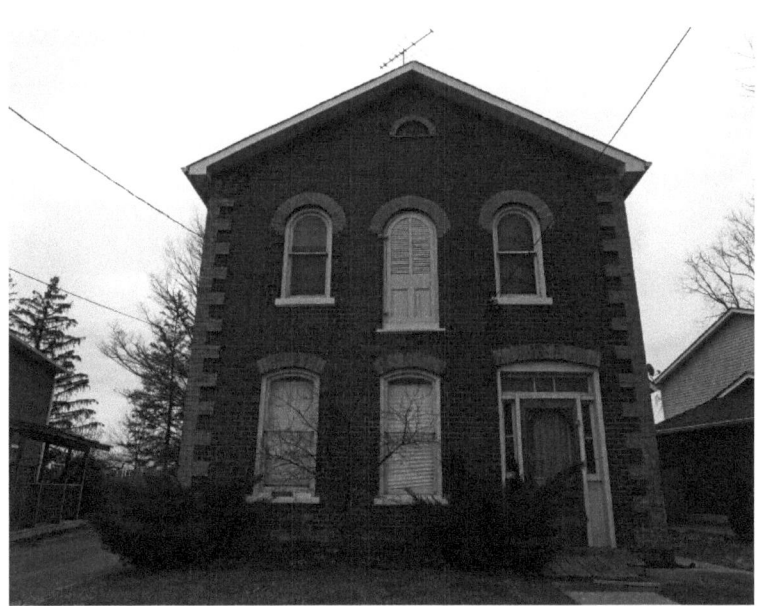

26 Caithness Street – Gothic Revival – corner quoins, arched window voussoirs

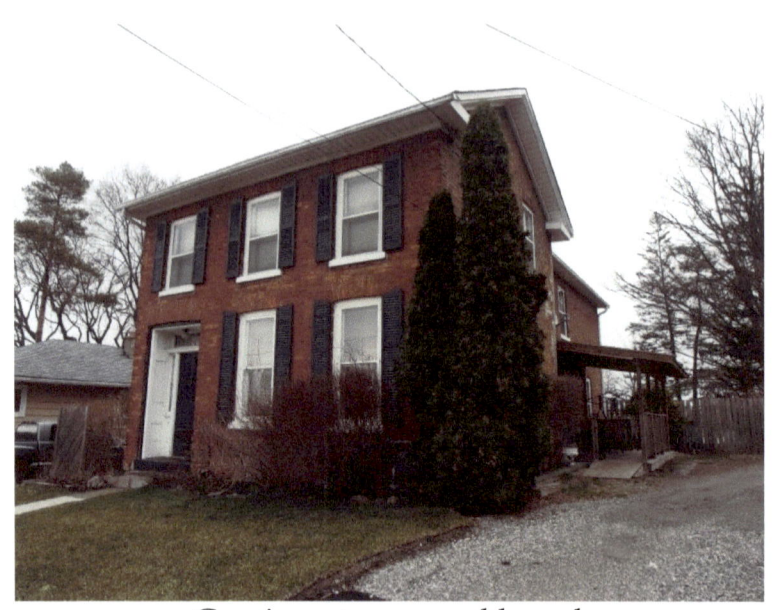

Cornice return on gable end

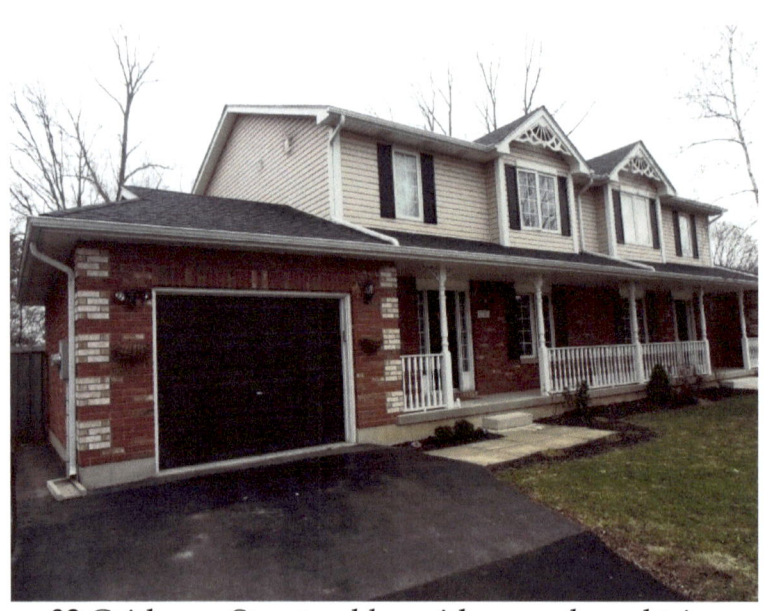

32 Caithness Street gables with verge board trim

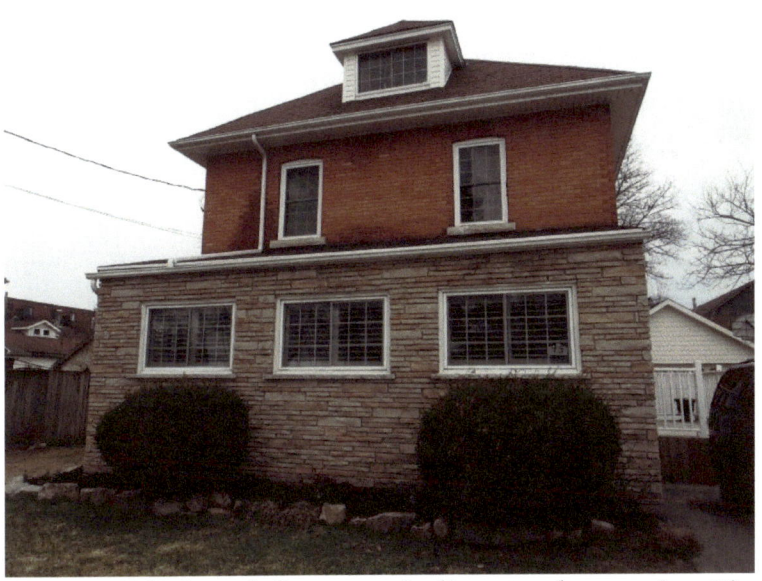

45 West Edinburgh Square – Italianate, dormer in attic, upgraded stonework on first storey

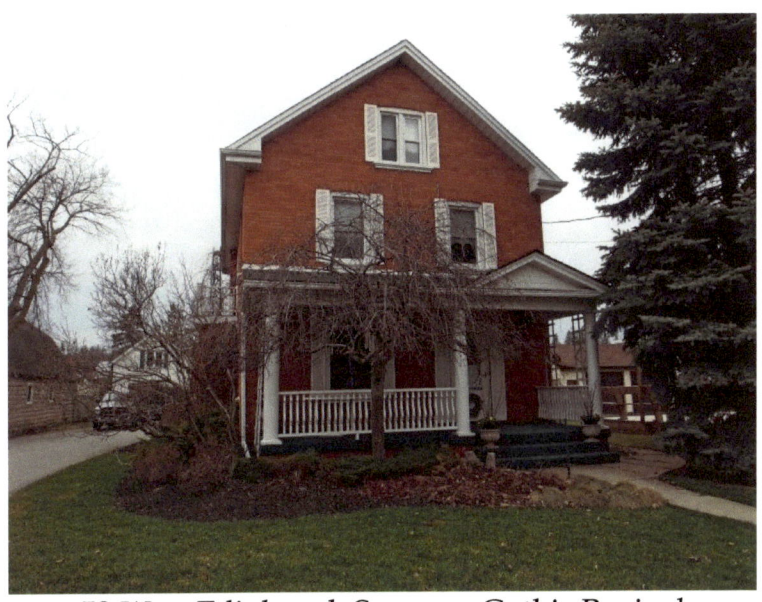

53 West Edinburgh Square – Gothic Revival

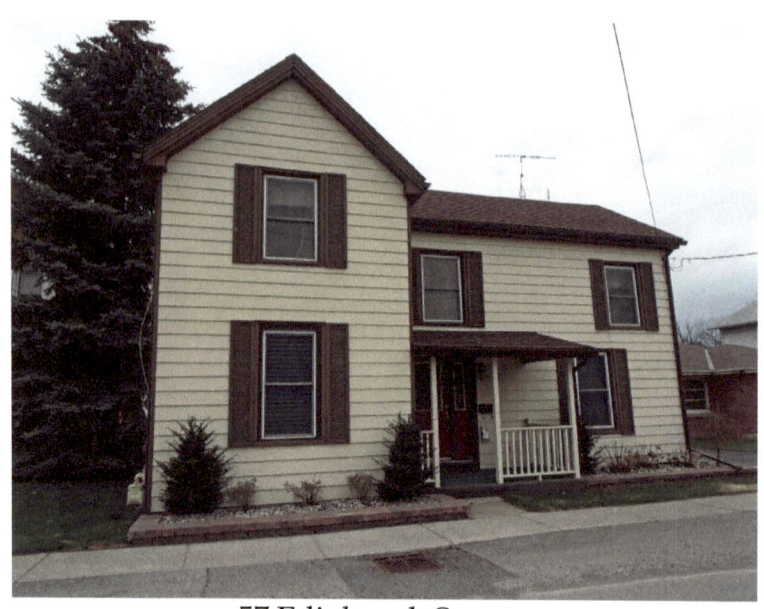

57 Edinburgh Square

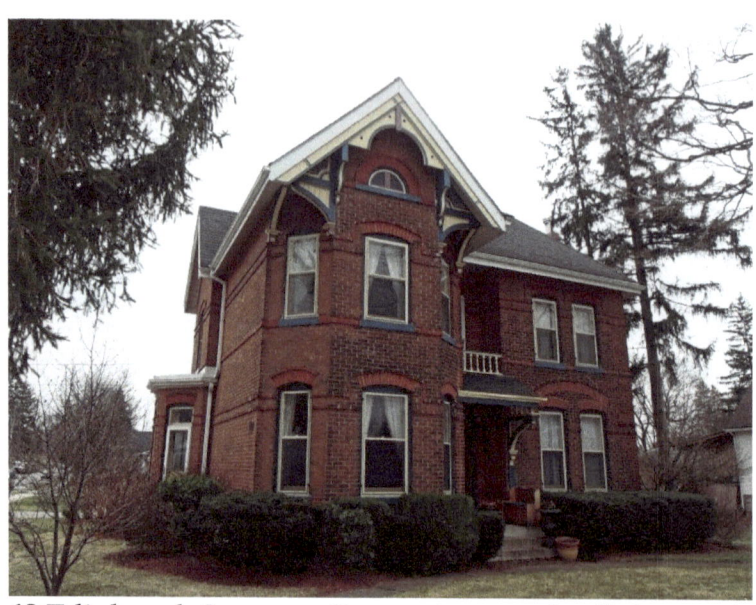

68 Edinburgh Square – Queen Anne style, dichromatic brickwork, verge board trim on two-and-a-half storey tower-like bay

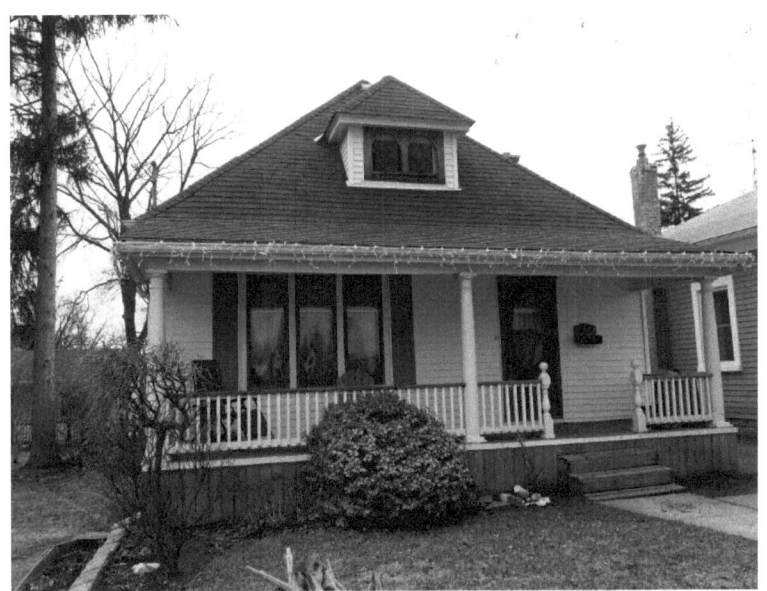

60 Edinburgh Square – one-and-a-half storey cottage with dormer in attic

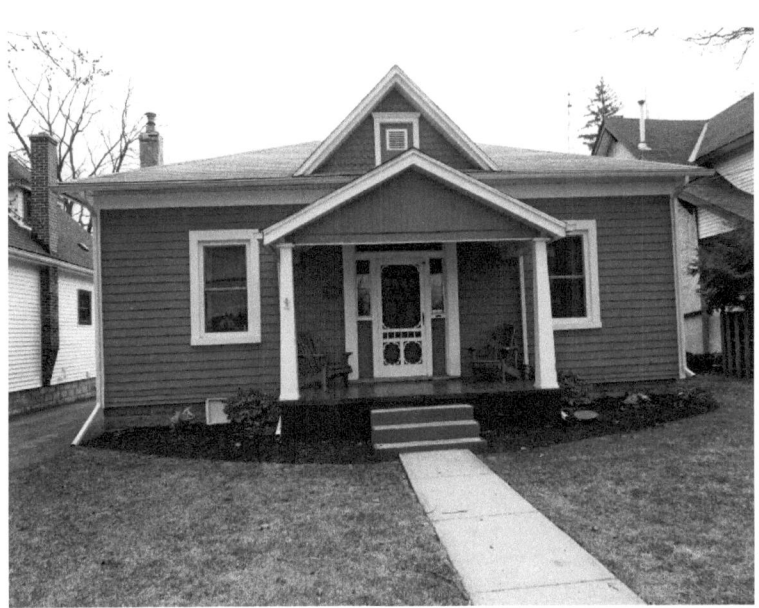

56 Edinburgh Square – Regency Cottage

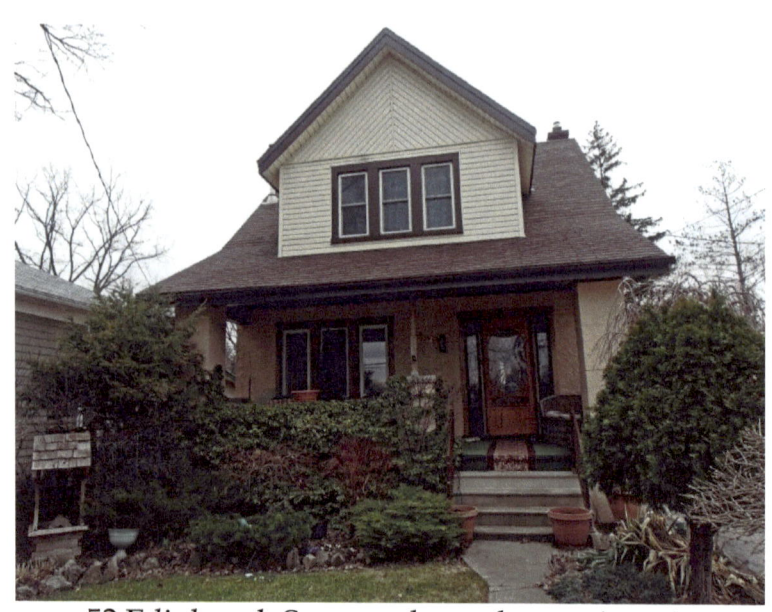

52 Edinburgh Square – large dormer in attic

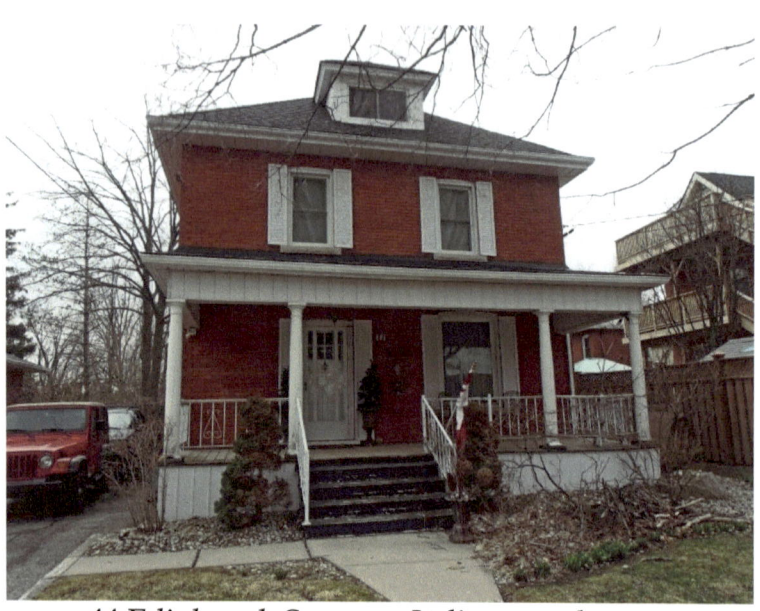

44 Edinburgh Square – Italianate - dormer

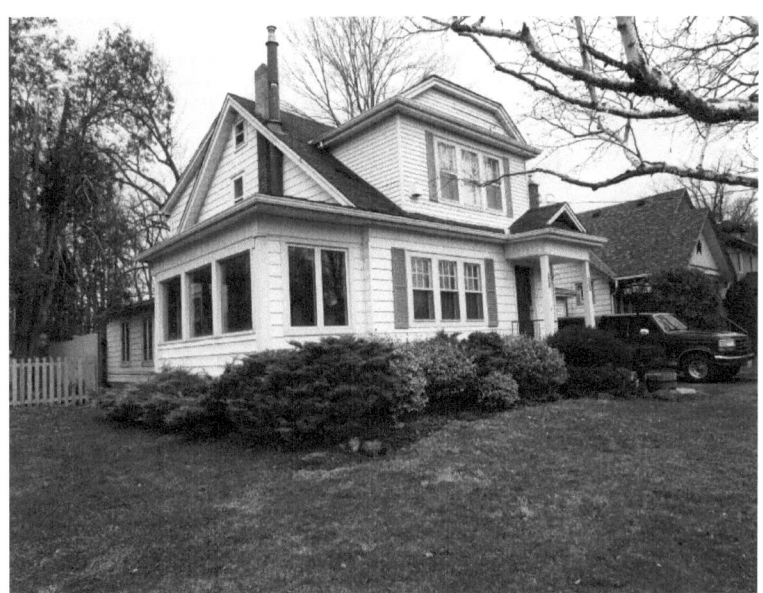

45 Banff Street

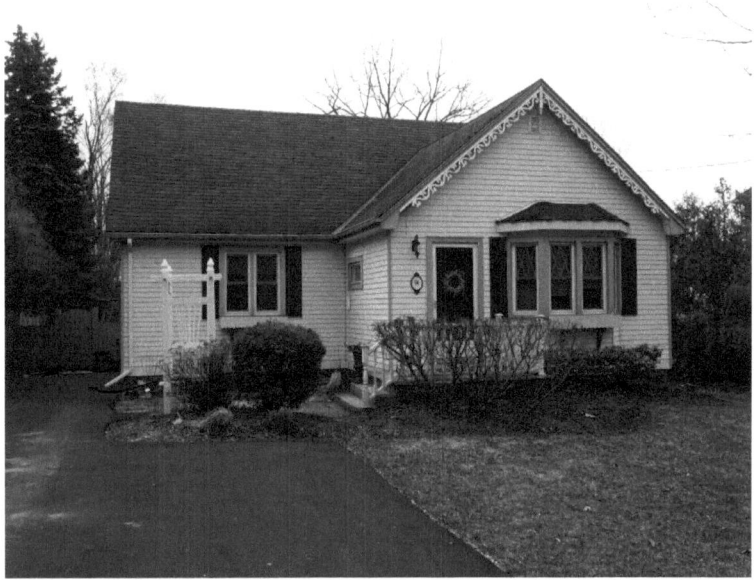

94 Banff Street – verge board trim and finial on gable, bay window

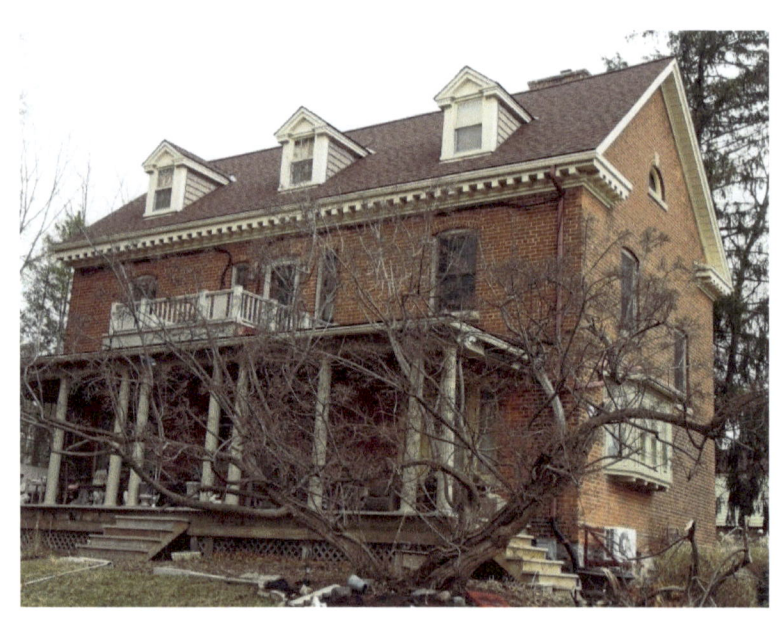

97 Banff Street – Gothic Revival - dormers in attic
Second floor balcony above verandah

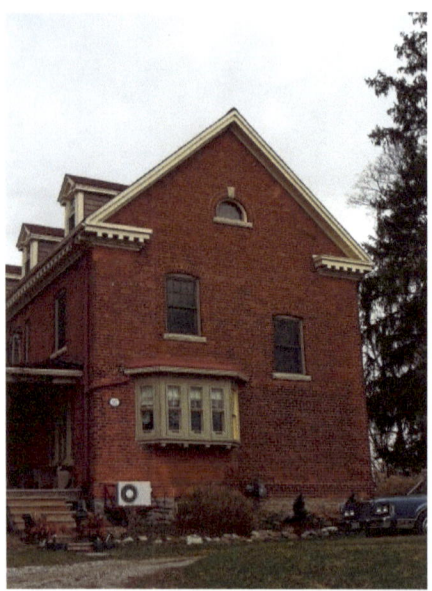

From end – cornice return on gable

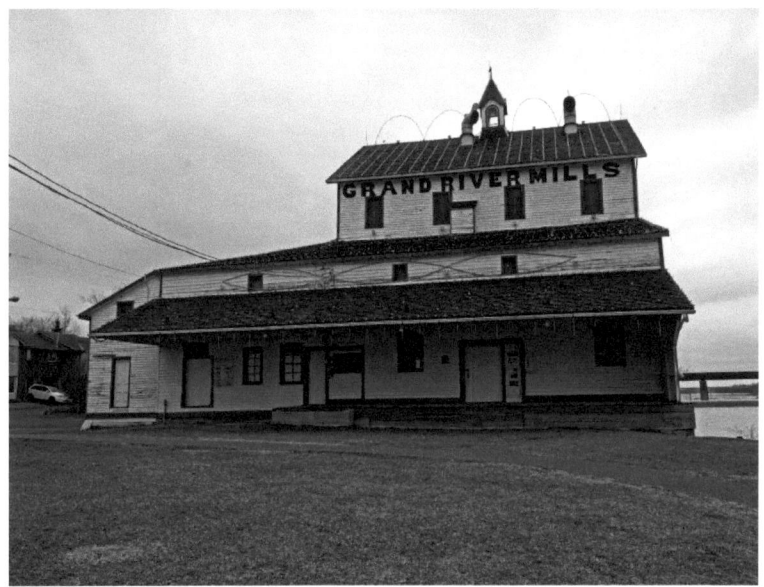

Grand River Mills – Caledonia Milling Co. – built in 1846 - the last timber-frame water powered mill along the Grand River in Ontario

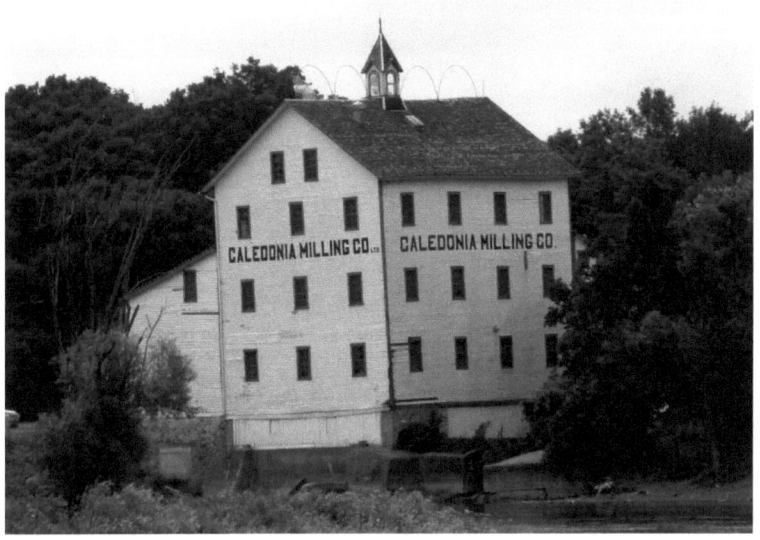

Forfar Street

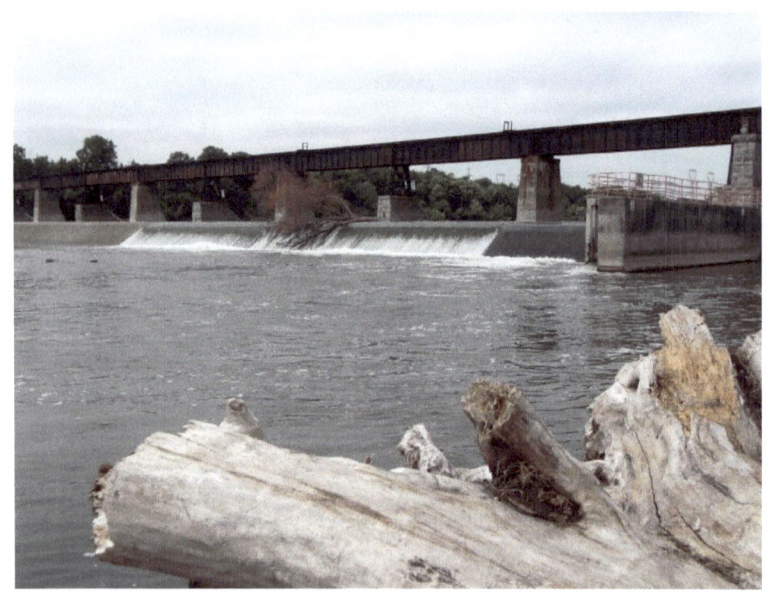

Caledonia dam

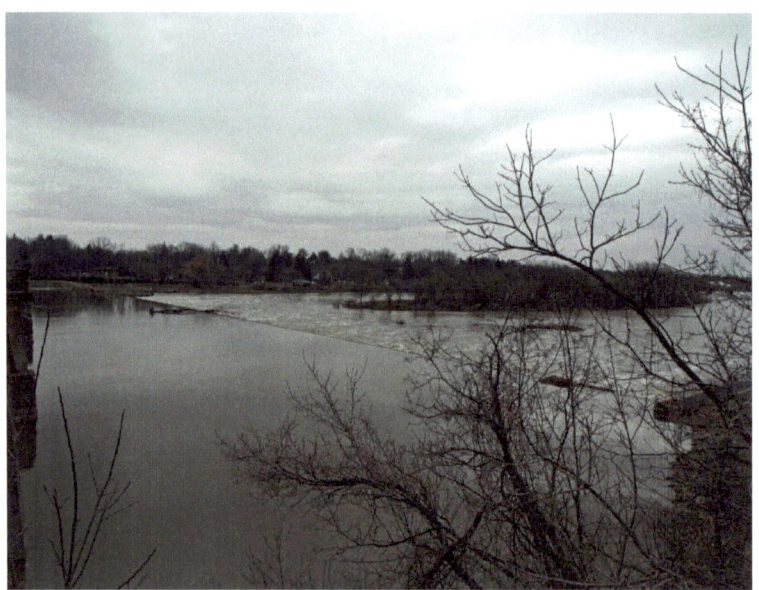

From above

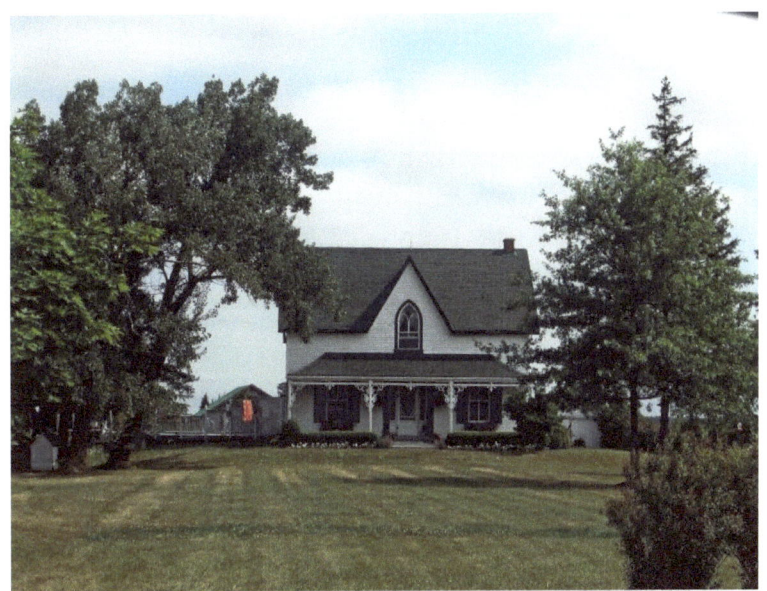

Gothic Revival Cottage

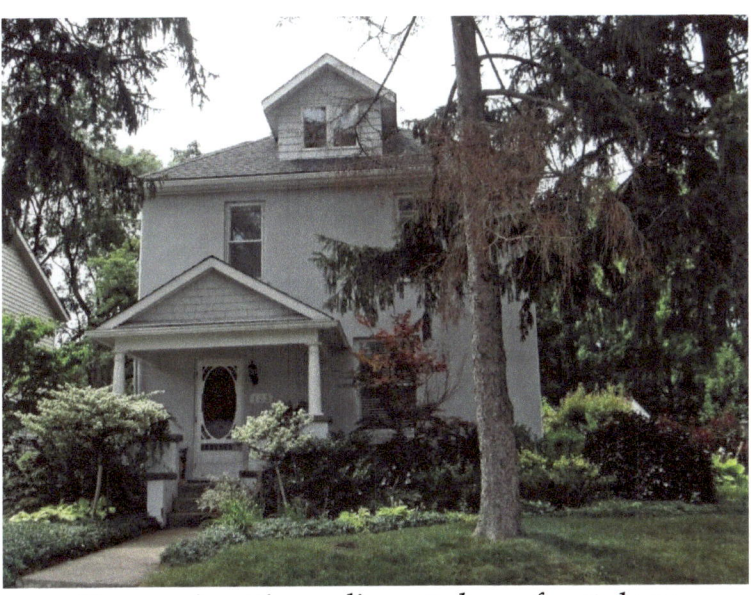

Dormer in attic, pediment above front door

Architectural Terms

Brackets: a decorative or weight-bearing structural element which forms a right angle with one side against a wall and the other under a projecting surface such as an eave or roof. Example: 149 Argyle Street	
Buttress: a masonry structure built against or projecting from a wall which serves to support or reinforce the wall. In Canadian architecture, they are sometimes used for decoration. Example: Grace United Church, 174 Caithness Street East	
Cornice: originally the wooden overhang of the roof. With the use of stone, brick, iron and steel, the cornice is any projecting shelf at the top of a ceiling or roof. They can be very decorative. Example: 201 Argyle Street	
Cornice Return: decorative element on the end of a gable. Example: 97 Banff Street	
Dentil Moulding: an even series of rectangles used as ornamental decoration in cornices. Example: Town Hall, Caithness Street	

Dichromatic brickwork: the use of two colours of brick, tile or slate to decorate a façade. Example: Argyle Street	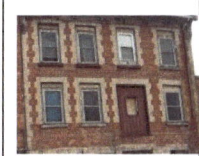
Dormer: (French for "sleep") a gable end window that pierces through the plane of a sloping roof surface to create usable space in the top floor or attic of a building by adding headroom. Example: 130 Caithness Street	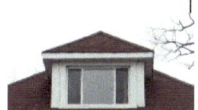
Gable: the triangular portion of a wall between the edges of a sloping roof. Example: 153 Argyle Street	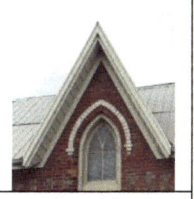
Hipped Roof: a roof where all sides slope downwards to the walls with no gables. Example: 96 Inverness Street	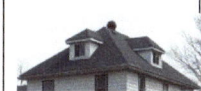
Keystones and Voussoirs: a voussoir is a wedge-shaped element used in building an arch. A keystone is the central stone that locks all the stones into position, allowing the arch to bear weight. A keystone is often enlarged and embellished. Example: 201 Argyle Street	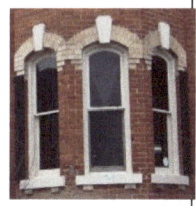

Lancet Window: a tall, narrow window with a pointed arch at its top. Example: Grace United Church, 174 Caithness Street East	
Palladian Window: a large window that is divided into three sections with the centre section larger than the two side sections and usually arched. Example: 94 Sutherland Street	
Pediment: a triangular section above the horizontal structure (entablature), typically supported by columns. The inside of the triangle is called the tympanum. Example: 129 Sutherland Street	
Quoin: masonry blocks at the corner of a wall, often a decorative feature, usually larger or of a different colour than the rest of the wall. Example: 201 Argyle Street	
Turret: a small tower that projects from the wall of a building. Example: 116 Caithness Street	
Verge boards: also called bargeboards – hang from the projecting end of a roof and are often elaborately carved and ornamented. Example: 204 Caithness Street	

Caledonia's Building Styles

Edwardian, 1900-1930 – This style bridges the ornate and elaborate styles of the Victorian era and the simplified styles of the 20th century. Balanced facades, simple roof lines, dormer windows, large front porches, and smooth brick surfaces are its characteristics. Example: 94 Sutherland Street	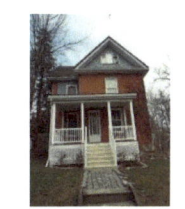
Georgian, before 1860 – This style began with the British King Georges in the 18th century. These buildings have balanced facades around a central door, medium-pitched gable roofs, and small paned windows. Example: Caithness Street, Town Hall	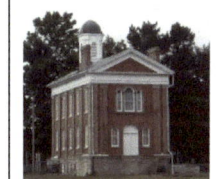
Gothic Revival, 1830-1890 – These decorative buildings have sharply-pitched gables with highly detailed verge boards, pointed-arch window openings, and dichromatic brickwork. It is a common style in Ontario. Example: 18 Orkney Street	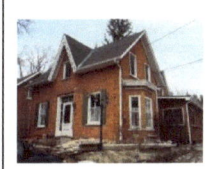
Italianate, 1850-1900 – It has wide-bracketed eaves, belvederes, wrap-around verandahs. Example: 201 Argyle Street	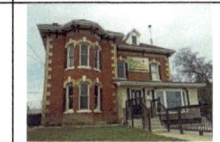
Regency Cottage, 1830-1860 – This style originated in England in 1815 and spread to Ontario later in the 19th century as British officers retired to Canada. It is a modest one-storey house with a low-pitched hip roof and has a symmetrical front façade. Example: Page 58	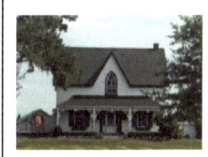

Other Books by Barbara Raue

Coins of Gold
Arrows, Indians and Love
The Life and Times of Barbara
The Cromwell Family Book
Laura Secord Discovered
Daddy Where Are You?

Montana Series
Book 1: Montana Dream
Book 2: Life on the Montana Frontier
Book 3: Montana to Boston and Back
Book 4: Montana Sons Go to War
Book 5: Montana Sons Return from War

Visit Barbara's website to view all of her books
http://barbararaue.ca

© 2018 by Barbara Raue - All the photos in this book have been taken with my cameras. I own the rights to them. I confirm that I will never submit any content for which I do not have the exclusive publishing rights. I will adhere to all terms in the Content Guidelines when publishing new content.